RADICAL
BUSINESS

RADICAL
BUSINESS

The Root of Your Work and
How It Can Change the World

DAVID GAINES

THE
collective.
BOOK STUDIO

Library of Congress Cataloging-in-Publication Data available.
ISBN: 978-1-68555-008-0
Ebook ISBN: 978-1-68555-009-7
Library of Congress Control Number: 2021924395

Printed using stock from sustainably managed forests.
Manufactured in China.

Cover and interior design by Andrea Kelly.
Typesetting by Maureen Forys, Happenstance Type-O-Rama.

1 3 5 7 9 10 8 6 4 2

The Collective Book Studio®
Oakland, California
www.thecollectivebook.studio

To my sons, Parker and Lincoln. I dream of a better world that you'll grow up into. I believe that a better world will exist, because younger people like you will be guiding us as we usher in a new economy that serves everyone.

Contents

Foreword

Some business leaders have forged new economies where there were previously none. They saw a gap and brought to life ideas that were likely considered outlandish. Others have permanently altered existing economies by taking a concept and building something so unique or valuable that we simply never went back to the way it was.

Transitions from the agrarian economy to industrial to service and experience were all the result of business leaders developing within a postconventional wisdom mindset. There are people who do not wear bike helmets because they simply do not want to. These people reject conventional wisdom. We can call them preconventional thinkers. There are people who wear bike helmets because it will keep them safe. They accept the conventional knowledge related to helmet safety. Next, we have the people who desire to move beyond what is conventionally accepted. These people wonder how to design a better bike helmet.

Using the same metaphor, I can best describe David's work as creating a world where we build a better bike helmet. In the process, he also wants to reconsider the manufacturing to ensure we are eliminating unnecessary and long-lasting impacts on our climate, ensure no one is disproportionately profiting off people's need for basic safety, and consider the ways that the company might curate a rich community through its employees and customers. There is the bike helmet, and then there is the entire ecosystem surrounding the production of that commodity. David exhibits postconventional wisdom with endurance and dedication like very few people I know.

Leaders like David energize me. I have many colleagues who are asking the same questions about how we can do better, but it ends with their curiosity. There is a plethora of thought leaders to pontificate on this ideology without delivering actual outcomes. David, however, has not just asked better questions and presented at conferences. He has created better products and, in the process, curated business practices that disrupt the status quo.

Where other leaders seek success by securing their market share in a specific industry, hoping for a profitable company and personal gain, David has ensured that every life impacted by his business is better because of it. Where some leaders follow the pathways forged by others in similar industries, maybe wishing they could do more for people or planet, or the community, David pioneers new pathways so that every business that comes after can build better.

Since we met several years ago and shared our desire for improved, lasting, and legitimate outcomes, we have been strong advocates for each other's work. We have sought each other's counsel. We have shared bold ideas for feedback on how to bring them to life. We have sent text requests for pep talks on exceptionally hard days. We are in each other's corner. You need someone in your corner if you're going to do this work. You are living a countercultural existence. Many people will look at you, sigh heavily, and ask if you can please just wear the bike helmet—as it is currently designed and be grateful for it.

David will be the first to tell you that this postconventional, countercultural work is exactly the work that he and everyone else should be doing. He will also tell you that he never realized it would be so hard to do the right thing. That is why this book exists. We cannot have just a handful of business leaders who are fighting against the odds and forging new paths. We need a collective movement. But in order for that to happen, we have to have more leaders step up and take this road less traveled.

This book is a map for this journey, leading the way for daring business leaders to follow. You are now a part of the community David is building. This book is a pep talk on a day that was exceptionally harder than it needed to be. This book is a reminder that better is possible and profitable.

My husband's great-grandfather was a dairy farmer. In those days, farmers delivered their milk in wagons drawn by horses. Then the car came along. Certain that the automobile was a fad, he never invested in a new business model. He quickly lost his market share. The neighboring farm, which did invest in milk trucks, quickly scaled their success. Today, that same neighboring farm is the dominant dairy farmer in a tri-state region. I actually had the opportunity to consult on their employee well-being strategy. It was the status quo. By that, I mean their model focused on reducing corporate financial risk by managing employees' personal health behavior. It is a company built on conventional business thinking.

I ask myself, what if my husband's great-grandfather saw the value of the car for his business and the impact it would have on reduced physical labor for his employees? What if he reinvested his increased revenue into better livestock care and management? What if he used the car to reach more homes and, in doing so, created a co-op to lower the price of milk for everyone? Would his farm have been the one to survive? If it did, what if he would have supported his neighbor's farm and expanded the company to ensure everyone had jobs? What if he did all that and still lost to the neighboring farm? Would it have been worth it for how it affected a communal mindset about what a great company could be?

If you have been asking yourself similar questions about how we work and lead in our present day, you will undoubtedly be energized by David's approach and the solutions you will find in this book.

—MAGGIE GOUGH, Chief Operating Officer, WELCOA

Introduction

When I hear someone talking about a "radical business idea," I expect to hear about something no one has done before—a brand-new concept, a new technology, or a new way of operating. Imagine my surprise when I found out that the primary definition of "radical" is actually the opposite of cutting-edge or innovative. Rather, it means "of or going to the root or origin." It comes from the Latin word *rādīcālis,* meaning "having roots," which came from the Latin *rādix,* or "root." This is where we get the word for radish, the root vegetable.

A "radical business," therefore, is not necessarily a business that's making crazy strides forward in terms of technology, innovation, and creative ideas—although that very well may be part of it. Instead, a truly "radical" business is one that goes back to its root purpose: to meet a need for a customer, to solve a problem, and to provide value.

This reframing of the word "radical" led me to the question, "What is the fundamental definition of 'work' and what is it supposed to be?" I believe that at the depth of our being, we are all creators, and I love to think that work in its purest, radical essence is to form, shape, and create. To be human is to celebrate the work of our hands.

We are seeing a reframing of work and business that has led us to a gateway moment in history. Our work can be used to not only restore a broken world but also to bring a sustainability to the planet and to our lives. But it's also bigger than that. I see a world beyond just sustaining our needs, one that is thriving in growth and beauty. I know that this is a radical notion, but I believe that businesses with social impacts can empower all people to be the best versions of themselves and help our planet flourish.

Imagine what it would look like when our collective work is all in line to make this world a better place! Leading a team or company, designing new and innovative products; helping to build systems that empower others; broadening our world view to include people with different experiences, backgrounds, and cultures; and conquering huge challenges like climate change; these are all ways we can make a positive impact in our world through work. Every job is a solution to a problem, and they all play a role in making this world a better place.

For as long as I can remember, I've held to this notion. As a young person, processes and problem-solving came naturally to me and I would often find myself investigating the systems around me, trying to figure out what was working and what wasn't. I was always full of ideas about how to improve this or edit that in order to make the whole thing run better, which is perhaps one of the most essential requirements for an entrepreneur or business owner.

As a child, problem-solving skills became most evident through my experience in Boy Scouts, which was the first place I felt empowered to learn and to lead others. An important part of my story is knowing that I was an outsider at school. I was a scrawny little kid—when I graduated from high school, I was six feet tall, weighing 150 pounds dripping wet. I had buck teeth, wasn't good at sports, and struggled with self-confidence.

Boy Scouts offered me an opportunity that school couldn't. In my third year, I became the leader of my patrol—a subsection of the larger Scout troop. The other members of this patrol? They were the misfits like me. Leadership and ingenuity were always within me and this was my first real chance to put those skills to use. So, at twelve years old, I decided to look past my patrol members' perceived weaknesses, choosing instead to identify each of our strengths and use them to our advantage as we worked toward completing various challenges. And guess what? Our little patrol started breaking records, even winning an award that had never before been earned in our troop history. We became one of the best-performing patrols in the whole city and even earned the respect of the older and "cooler" patrols.

At such a formative age, this experience taught me an important lesson that has shaped me as a social entrepreneur today. I was able to pull together a group of fellow nerds, cast a vision, and do some really cool things—both for the members of my patrol and also for my community.

Despite my feelings of being on the outside looking in, I also recognize that I am extremely privileged in so many ways, as a white, American, straight man. I grew up lower-middle class, so my family was by no means wealthy, but we had enough. There was always food on the table and we were never hungry. I was able to get my teeth fixed, which was an expensive, mostly cosmetic (and therefore optional) procedure that gave me an entirely new level of confidence. As fortunate as I was, I also have an idea of what it's like to be an outsider, to be deemed as less worthy, to be a member of the "have-nots." And I also experienced firsthand what can happen when those in ostracized groups are empowered: really amazing things.

I continued to become a more involved Scout leader until I graduated from high school. The natural inclination to notice and improve the systems around me continued when I was an adult. I remember, for example, the first time I ate at Chipotle. I was not only impressed with my very tasty burrito, I was also excited about the company's decision to use pure ingredients at an accessible price. However, I also remember noticing a few pain points during that first visit. The cashier, for instance, seemed to be the bottleneck in the ordering process, inhibiting the number of customers they could serve within a certain amount of time—a problem a frequent Chipotle customer experiences. As I sat and ate my burrito, I found myself redesigning the restaurant's flow in my mind, with the idea of creating a more positive and efficient experience for both customers and employees.

As a young adult, my pull toward entrepreneurship became even stronger for another reason: freedom. I was willing to work hard, but I wanted to be free from the obligation to work on someone else's schedule and for someone else's agenda. Alongside my love of business was a strong urge to actively impact the world in a positive way. It would be years before I realized that I could do both at the same time. Back then, I believed that "work" had to be separate from "positive impact," and therefore I saw entrepreneurship as a means to an end: if I could be my own boss, then I could flex my time and energy in order to volunteer in my community as much as I wanted. Not only that, but I also desired more earning potential so that I could one day use the funds from my business to do something with a greater purpose. Entrepreneurship could give me the time and financial freedom to make a difference in a way that was most meaningful to me.

My dreams of becoming my own boss began to materialize at the age of twenty when I got the opportunity to start an environmentally conscious carpet-cleaning business. I had been working at Wendy's while in college when a manager who trusted my work ethic approached me with an idea. The restaurant's owners were having problems with their contracted carpet-cleaning company and they had yet to find a replacement. My manager suggested that I offer to take on the job myself. I gratefully took the opportunity and ran with it, full speed. After proving myself at one restaurant, I was referred to another location, and then another. After about nine months, I was able to gain enough clientele through word-of-mouth referrals to become my own full-time boss.

I had begun this crazy journey of owning my own business. To call it a "small business" would be a stretch—most of the time, I just worked by myself. But I had achieved what I set out to do: I had the time and financial freedom to volunteer when I could, and on my terms. So, for the next fifteen years, that's exactly what I did. I was heavily involved in a couple of community organizations where I used my time and energy to do things like organize food drives and mentor younger people. I was able to provide both practical and intellectual resources that could help empower others in my local and global community.

Of course, the satisfaction of reaching my initial goals lasted only so long, and my ambitions began to change. I had created a job for myself that paid the bills and allowed me to be as involved as I wanted in social causes I cared about, but it wasn't a business that I had grown beyond myself. As I grew older, I wanted more. Instead of volunteering, I wanted to be able to actually scale my company and provide sustainable jobs for people. I wanted to increase my financial contributions to issues near and dear to me. I wanted to build something that was bigger than just me, literally and metaphorically. But I wasn't able to do any of this because my current way of operating had plateaued. My business had reached a point where I couldn't grow without investing more time, energy, and finances in hiring and running a larger team. However, I couldn't do that without sacrificing the very thing I had built my business for in the first place: my volunteer time. I felt stuck. I had to choose between the two: grow my business or continue with my nonprofit work.

I knew that solution to my problem was somewhere out there—I just had to find it. As I brainstormed what could be next for my life and career, I devoured countless books on subjects like team building, leadership, branding, company culture, and more. I applied as many of these lessons to my business as I could, but there was a larger idea brewing underneath it all that would change the trajectory of my career.

My Introduction to Coffee

As I grew my carpet-cleaning business in my twenties and thirties, a friend of mine named Chuck had also started a business of his own: La Terza Coffee, a specialty coffee roasterie in Cincinnati, Ohio. This wasn't just any coffee company—it was the highest quality coffee you could find within driving distance of my house. I knew there was something very different about this coffee because I actually enjoyed it. At the time I was the furthest thing from a coffee connoisseur—I didn't like coffee, I didn't drink coffee, and I had no desire to start. But for some reason, what my friend Chuck was making was a different experience.

Like so many entrepreneurs and artisans, Chuck was incredibly talented, knowledgeable, and passionate about his craft, but his business was going through a lot of changes and he had become overwhelmed. Having been through many of these branding and structural shifts with my own business, I offered to help Chuck as a consultant.

As we got into the weeds of the company, I also realized that Chuck's work was more than your typical small business—it was a for-profit business but was also dedicated to helping other people. By simply operating and having a relationship with coffee producers and importers, he was having a very tangible impact around the world. At the time, La Terza was one in a small percentage of coffee companies that was operating fairly and ethically inside an industry that was fraught with injustice.

As I witnessed firsthand how a traditional business could also have social impact, the seed that had been planted in my mind earlier began to slowly but surely take root: maybe I didn't have to choose between building a profitable company and having a positive impact on my community. In fact, perhaps it was not only possible to do both at the same time, but it could potentially be even more powerful than if I tried to keep the two divorced from one another.

Over time, my role slowly and organically expanded beyond business consultant. After about a year, it began to make sense for me to actually buy the business from Chuck and become the primary owner. It was a well-suited transition for both of us: my work would consist of running the aspects of the business that I was passionate about and gifted in—business development and social impact—and Chuck's work would be focused where his talent and dedication lay— phenomenal coffee and building relationships. So, in 2013, I began the journey to transition out of my carpet-cleaning business and fully focus my energy with La Terza Coffee.

It didn't take long for the business to start growing. We added a few other part-owners whose strengths lay where mine and Chucks didn't—like the legal and accounting departments—to put together a solid team. We even managed to attract some incredible coffee talent within the barista community.

Within the first year, we began rebuilding the foundation of a business that would one day go beyond Chuck and me. Along with my team, I was on my way to having a real, measurable, and scalable positive impact on the world, but through a for-profit business model. "Social enterprise" was not yet in my vocabulary, but I was able to see clearly that "profitability" and "positive impact" didn't have to be separate from one another. The more coffee La Terza sold and the more it grew as a company, the larger impact it could make in the

DEFINING QUALITY

In most professions, the operator's skill, experience, education, and budget give the customer different options of quality to choose from. There are many coffee shops and restaurants that rely on coffee and espresso equipment that can be programmed to make drinks at a push of a button. At this type of coffee shop, the barista making your drink behind the coffee bar just needs a basic understanding of coffee in order to make a great tasting drink. On the other end of the spectrum, there are coffee shops where everything is hand-crafted. Drinks are made with a higher level of artisanship, care, and detail, and the experience of the customer is much more unique. For this kind of barista, there are even opportunities to compete and hone your skills against other baristas around the world. Shortly after I began working at La Terza full-time, a man named Robert Gatesi had moved to Cincinnati from Uganda and was looking for work in the coffee industry. Robert's reputation preceded him. He was an African Barista Champion and had competed in three World Barista Championships. Today, Robert is our Master Roaster.

world by building direct relationships with farmers and paying them fair rates for their beans. Those farmers are then able to reinvest in their workers, families, and communities, creating a ripple effect of positive impact.

Seeing the potential in La Terza gave me hope and began a transition toward true integrity for me. The word "integrity" comes from the word "integer," which means "one." I'd always wanted to be someone who lives with integrity, but I'd always felt split and divided within myself. I worked like I had to always choose between making money and investing in social causes. As I slowly learned about the social enterprise concept, I began to feel more whole. I didn't have to split up my work, goals, values, or core identity. I gradually began to feel more like the truest version of me. What I realized is that I was becoming radical with myself . . . moving to the roots of who I have always been. And this feeling would profoundly impact the rest of my career.

Throughout this book, I've used many examples, statistics, and references. In an effort to minimize the environmental impact of the paper used for the book's printing, you can find references at www.radicalbizbook.com/references.

Some Social Enterprise-Adjacent Terms

Below is a list of terms that you will probably come across in the world of social enterprise. Many of them are related, even almost synonymous, so I've included a brief description of each to provide some clarity.

Social impact business: A broad term used to describe a for-profit entity that addresses a pressing social challenge in an impactful way.

Positive impact business: Can be used synonymously with social impact business.

Social entrepreneurship: The idea of social impact business, but applied specifically to start-up companies.

Conscious capitalism: A term coined and popularized by John Mackey, the co-founder of Whole Foods, and Raj Sisodia, a researcher, professor, and author. (The two collaborated on the book *Conscious Capitalism: Liberating the Heroic Spirit of Business.*) Conscious capitalism refers to for-profit organizations that prioritize both profit and positive impact, and therefore excludes nonprofit and governmental organizations.

Accountability capitalism: Comes from the Accountability Capitalism Act, a proposed federal bill introduced by Senator Elizabeth Warren in 2018. The act includes a "constituency statute" that would give companies a duty of "creating a general public benefit" with regard to all of its short- and long-term stakeholders, which would include not only shareholders but also employees, the environment, and so on.

Conscious consumer: Someone who considers the who and how behind a product, and who bases purchasing decisions on the perceived positive or negative impact a certain product or service has on the world. Conscious consumers are people who "vote with their dollar" in an attempt to push the entire market toward more responsible and ethical operation.

Triple bottom line: Refers to "people, planet, and profit." Calling an organization a triple bottom line business is a condensed way of communicating that the business prioritizes all of its stakeholders equally, as opposed to insisting on profit overall.

Ethical brand/business: Often refers to the "people" part of "people, planet, profit." Generally, an "ethical brand" or "ethically made product" indicates that the people involved in the supply chain work in safe conditions, are not overworked, are paid a living wage, and receive other benefits such as health care, education, and sick pay.

Sustainable brand/business: Generally refers to the "planet" part of "people, planet, profit." Producing a "sustainable product" makes a minimal footprint on our environment. Sustainable products are made from natural, biodegradable, nontoxic, and/or recycled materials; use low-impact processes; utilize things like carbon offsets and plastic-free shipping and the like. The terms "ethical" and "sustainable" can sometimes be used interchangeably, as you often cannot truly have one without the other.

Corporate social responsibility (CSR): A social impact program within a traditional business or corporation. These programs can have a significant social impact but are not typically part of the primary purpose of the business. Sometimes these initiatives are temporary, to address immediate needs within communities, but more businesses are incorporating many long-term goals and initiatives as a way to be more active participants within their local and global communities.

Benefit Corporation or B-Corp: A third-party certification that assesses the overall positive impact of a company. For a list of other common ethical and sustainable certifications, see pages 58–61.

Impact investing: Investments "made into companies, organizations, and funds with the intention to generate a measurable, beneficial, social or environmental impact alongside a financial return" (The Global Impact Investing Network).

PART 1

The New Economy Is Coming

Our culture, and the economy that goes with it, are entering a new era. The younger generations of consumers— millennials, members of Gen Z, and now Gen Alpha—have growing expectations that the companies they work for and the products and services they purchase from are thinking about doing business in a way that is more holistic; thinking of how companies are engaging with all of humanity and the planet. These young citizens are becoming more socially and politically active. They're voting with their dollars. They're holding companies to a higher standard. They're embracing the idea of capitalism with a conscience.

It's been over two centuries since the Industrial Revolution, when the productivity and profit of capitalism began to sky-rocket. Although we have many great things thanks to our current economic system, we are also seeing the disadvantages and lack of sustainability of what psychologist and author Tim Kasser calls "hyper-capitalism," or others may call "late capitalism."

Our economy's dependence on fossil fuels has created an unprecedented climate crisis. The wage gap between the rich and poor, which has been even further exacerbated by the COVID-19 pandemic, keeps widening. When adjusted for inflation, the minimum wage in 2022 was less than it was in 1956. Along with a myriad of other ethical issues, countless companies have been found guilty of using human trafficking and slave labor to produce the goods we buy, use, eat, and wear. The largest and most powerful corporations are able to invade citizens' privacy with little to no consequences. And what was once a system built on empowering anyone to reach for their dreams, capitalism has turned into a system that relies on overconsumption, consumer debt, environmental destruction, and modern-day slavery. These practices are sustained by the exploitation of human dissatisfaction and ill-health through the constant bombardment of marketing.

The American economic system has been divided into three main segments: for-profit, nonprofit, and government. Each was designed to play a distinct role, with for-profits generating revenue, government serving the public infrastructures like education and transportation, and nonprofits serving people in the margins and the different perspectives of religion and morality. Because of this basic framework, many have argued for decades that it is not the role of business to address society's moral shortcomings and that they belong in the nonprofit sector and our religious institutions.

However, we are entering a new era. Business is evolving and our relationship to work is changing. We have reached a point where the "moral" and the "profitability" cannot be so easily separated. Consumers, shareholders, and CEOs alike are now calling for social responsibility and profitability to exist alongside one another. In August 2019, 181 of the largest companies, from Apple and Walmart to Vanguard and Goldman Sachs, released the "Statement of the Purpose of a Corporation" through the Business Roundtable. The purpose was to "supersede" previous statements that "stated that corporations exist principally to serve their shareholders."

In this updated declaration, the CEOs drastically widened the definition of "stakeholder" to include not only those who put a stake in their companies with direct investment dollars, but also those who do so with their time and energy (employees and suppliers), with their trust and buying dollars (customers), and with their participation in the larger free market (communities and environment). All these stakeholders together are necessary for corporations to operate. "Each of our stakeholders is essential," the statement concludes. "We commit to deliver value to all of them, for the future success of our companies, our communities, and our country."

This statement of purpose reflects a monumental and meaningful change in the way we might collectively approach business. There is a new type of economy coming, and the companies that don't adjust and adapt will be left behind. Organizations that don't listen to the demands of younger consumers will fail. No longer can businesses operate in an ethical way simply because "it's the right thing to do" morally speaking. It is now the right thing to do in terms of the bottom line, too. Even those entrepreneurs and business leaders who couldn't care less about issues like modern-day slavery and climate change should realize that we are ushering in a new way, and that if they are going to continue to turn a profit, radical responsibility has to be at the forefront of their business plans.

Which leads me to hope.

I believe we can use many of the same tools that got us into our current predicament to get us out of it and move toward a more equitable and sustainable future. After all, in their essence, businesses are built to solve problems for a customer. So, who's to say they can't also be used to solve larger societal problems like inequality, environmental destruction, and even employee burnout? This book is not about getting rid of capitalism—it's about how businesses can usher in a newer, better form of capitalism in a practical way.

Although this book is primarily geared toward small- and medium-sized business owners, managers, and entrepreneurs, its contents can help just about anyone make a larger positive impact in their personal life, business, activism, and/or creative work. If you work for a large corporation, you can find ways to implement positive social impact within your department. If you dream of being an entrepreneur one day, you can use this book as a holistic framework so that when the day comes, you're able to start your business off on the right foot. If you run or work for a nonprofit organization, most of this content will easily apply to your work as well.

You can even apply the principles of social entrepreneurship to your own life as an individual consumer and citizen in how you spend your money. Every dollar we spend supports the organizations we purchase from. Conversely, our voices are also heard where we don't spend money—both in our small daily purchases as well as moments of organized boycotting. Every dollar spent is a vote, and as more companies incorporate social initiatives in their work, we are showing our support with our purchasing power.

The idea of a social enterprise is not new. Nowadays there are tons of positive-impact companies out there, with new ones popping up every day—which I'm so excited about. Things have changed a lot in the past ten to fifteen years. Prior to the 2010s, most organizations in the US had to make a clear choice between becoming a nonprofit or for-profit entity. When I discovered that La Terza was a for-profit company making a social impact—blurring the lines between for profit and nonprofit—I wondered: How many other "do-good" businesses are out there that I don't know about?

Of course, I knew of TOMS Shoes, which had been founded a few years earlier. With their "Buy One, Give One" model and incredible marketing campaigns, TOMS proved that it's possible to do good while turning a profit at the same time, paving the way for the current generation of social impact businesses. I also knew plenty of large corporations that implemented some sort of corporate social responsibility (CSR) initiative, where they'd give back a portion of their profits to a charity organization. The way I saw it however, there was a crucial difference between putting ethical responsibility at the core of operations and simply giving back a portion of profits or products. I couldn't help wondering if there were more companies that were going beyond the give-back model to operate in a more holistic and sustainable way.

This question eventually snowballed into other ones that began to bother me, like:

- What specifically constitutes a "good," "ethical," or "social impact" business?
- How do we define or measure "good" or "impact"?
- How do we hold companies to high standards in a practical way while also allowing room for improvement when "ethical perfection" may be unattainable?
- Which is more beneficial: a donation to someone in need or creating opportunities for dignified work?
- What about businesses that support social causes but are in direct opposition to social causes that I care about. Are they still considered social enterprises?
- In what areas must a company be making a positive impact in order to be considered a social enterprise?
- What about companies that sacrifice the quality of their product and use marketing to sell the "story" of their social impact rather than invest in a product you'd want to buy again and again?
- How do the roles of nonprofit, for-profit, and government organizations differ, and how might they work together?
- Is the idea of "conscious capitalism" even possible?

I realize now that these questions and ideas had been brewing inside me for a long time, just waiting to be asked, explored, clarified, and even continually edited. I still don't have the answers to all these questions, but through my work at La Terza, I've learned that there are many ways for a company to have a positive impact on the world.

The version of capitalism we've been operating under since the Industrial Revolution is dying. It's not working for us anymore, and we see proof of it every day. Some economists and scientists might argue that it has to die—or else it will kill us first. I don't say that to be dramatic or fear-mongering, but rather to encourage us to take an honest look at the direction we're headed in the hope that we might be able to make needed changes as soon as possible. The United Nations reported in July 2019 that one climate disaster (i.e., a tropical storm, drought, etc.) happens every single week somewhere around the world, costing us about $520 billion per year, and disaster frequency has been steadily increasing over time. Simply put, the current version of our economy cannot sustain the type of climate needed for the survival of the growing human race.

Not only that, today's consumers are fed up. The next generations of consumers don't want to spend their money on products and services from irresponsible companies that are operating out of line with their values. They want high-quality products at a fair price from brands that treat their workers and the planet with care. These younger consumers are the future; therefore, in the long run, what they say goes. Demand will continue to drive the market, and these young people are certainly demanding a new, different, and more responsible economy.

This change in generational expectations is a good thing, and I see it as an incredible opportunity. While it may seem like the huge corporations are taking over, the numbers tell us that small businesses are often the overlooked powerhouses of our economy, and that we can absolutely compete with large corporations and monopolies. In 2019, small businesses generated 44 percent of US economic activity. In 2017, almost half of the nation's private sector workforce (47.1%) were employed by small businesses. Over the past twenty-five years and throughout the economic recession brought from the COVID-19 pandemic, large businesses generated 6.7 million net new jobs while small businesses generated 12.9 million net new jobs, meaning that small businesses have accounted for two out of every three new jobs created. Even in the age of

COVID-19, with the fate of so many enterprises on the line, I still believe that small businesses can and will be the solution to so many of our current problems, just like they were following past recessions.

These are not small numbers. They remind me of an analogy that I heard once about ants and elephants. Let's think of small businesses as the ants and huge corporations as the elephants. At first glance, it may seem obvious that the elephants are significantly stronger, smarter, and more powerful than the ants. But when added together, the ants actually weigh a lot more. As of 2020, there are about 450,000 elephants in the world. An average adult elephant weighs about 8,800 to 14,000 pounds, depending on the species. So, if we use 11,500 pounds as the median, all the elephants in the world weigh somewhere around 2,587,500 tons.

The average ant weighs 2.5 milligrams, and scientists conservatively estimate that there are 20 quadrillion ants on Earth. That means the weight of all the ants on this planet is somewhere around 50 quadrillion milligrams. That's 55,115,565 tons. That means that all the ants added together weigh over 50 million tons more than all of the elephants! Needless to say, that's quite a significant difference.

The point is this: When we join forces as entrepreneurs, small business owners, managers, and team members, we can actually compete with the giant corporations to usher in this new economy. Together, we hold an incredible amount of power to move the needle toward a more positive, equitable, and sustainable future.

Section 1

What Is Social Enterprise, Anyway?

When I met my friend Maggie Gough, she had a small business that provided resources and education on employee well-being for companies of all shapes and sizes. Whether she was facilitating workshops with small groups or speaking to large audiences, Maggie was and continues to be dedicated to creating workplaces filled with thriving, healthy employees.

One day over lunch, I asked Maggie if she'd be interested in becoming a member of the Social Enterprise Alliance. SEA is a national network of organizations that seeks to empower social enterprises with the tools and resources they need to succeed. Because of the positive impact that Maggie's business was making in our community, it was an obvious fit for membership.

"What are you talking about?!" she asked me with surprise. "My business isn't a social enterprise."

"What are you talking about?" I asked. "Of course it is! You're directly improving the lives of employees who often feel underappreciated and burnt out. You're making vital, positive impacts that have ripple effects on our whole society."

Maggie was skeptical at first. The idea of "social enterprise" in her head involved charities or nonprofits, artisans in third-world countries, or second-chance workers here in the States. While Maggie very much saw the deep purpose of her work in helping employers design work for employee well-being, she didn't think she checked the boxes of a "social entrepreneur." But then I asked a question that Maggie had trouble answering. "How is your business not a social enterprise?"

Maggie is most certainly not alone. I've consulted and networked with hundreds of small business owners over the years, explaining to more than a few individuals that their businesses were in fact social enterprises—they just didn't know it. Either they simply hadn't heard of the idea of social enterprise, they believed they didn't fit the bill because they were trying to make a profit, or they were convinced that their small social initiative couldn't have a deep and long-lasting impact.

Back when I ran my green carpet-cleaning business, I had no idea I was owning and operating a social enterprise either. I was simply cleaning carpets. I did not take into account that we were using cleaning agents that were also safe for the customer, including their children and pets who often play and roll around on the floor. I did not think about how a significant part of our services in cleaning homes was educational for the homeowners, empowering them through education on how to improve indoor air quality and increase the life of their carpets. I didn't consider how we often donated portions of our proceeds toward clean water initiatives in other parts of the world. And I absolutely did not think about how the work enabled me to be involved in many other social causes. If I asked my younger self the same question I asked Maggie, "How are you not a social enterprise?" I would not have been able to answer the question. I know that mine and Maggie's experiences are not unusual. Maybe you own or work with a social enterprise even as you read this book, and you also haven't realized it yet.

Embracing the social enterprise "label" allows entrepreneurs like Maggie—who are often working alone and against cultural odds—to find a community of support; and with joining a larger community of social enterprise entrepreneurs comes a host of resources. Being a social enterprise, Maggie could develop herself and her business with greater breadth and depth than when she was doing it alone.

I believe that part of the reason Maggie, myself, and so many others have faced confusion about whether our organizations belong in the social enterprise category is that there isn't a universal consensus about what a social enterprise actually is. Not only that, but the loose definition we do have has expanded and evolved quite a bit since the turn of the century.

I would say that a social enterprise can be generally described as "an organization that considers all of the stakeholders involved in the business's operations (including members of the supply chain, employees, the environment, investors, etc.)." Stripped down to its most basic definition, one could say that a social enterprise is a business that does good. The challenge then is, how do we define "good" and how much "good" is enough to be a social enterprise? We all have our own thoughts and ideas about "good" and "good enough," which makes measuring and defining nearly impossible.

While it can be difficult to fully define what a social enterprise is, it's worth the effort to try. Even if they can sometimes be ambiguous, they are also useful guides to help us strive and grow toward deepening our impact.

The different definitions are similar in that they focus on social responsibility or solving a social problem. Social enterprises could also be described as "organizations that make a positive impact in the world in some way—whether through dignified job creation, environmental responsibility, and/or other initiatives." However, when you take this idea out of books and into real life, it can often raise more questions than it answers. Can both for-profits and nonprofits be considered social enterprises? What about organizations in the government sector? In what areas must a company be making a

SOCIAL ENTERPRISE AND CONSCIOUS BUSINESS

Here are a few examples of how different organizations in the industry have chosen to define the ideas of social enterprise and conscious business.

The **Social Enterprise Alliance** (SEA), as referenced above, defines a social enterprise as: "An organization created for impact. It uses a sustainable and earned income business model with a governing structure focused on stated social or environmental goals. It invests a significant portion of its revenue, profit, or assets into expanding this stated mission."

Conscious Capitalism, Inc., which is focused more on larger companies, says that "conscious businesses are galvanized by higher purposes that serve, align, and integrate the interests of all their major stakeholders." Those stakeholders include customers, employees, vendors, investors, communities, and others.

The **Center for Social Entrepreneurship at Miami University Oxford** defines social entrepreneurship as: "innovative solutions to persistent social problems—particularly to those that are marginalized or poor—that create social value through sustainable, systemic change."

Social Enterprise World Forum recognizes that defining what a social enterprise is can be a complex question to answer as there are many cultural and structural differences throughout the world. But they do offer that at the core, social enterprises have a mission focus, surplus aimed at helping the mission, ownership tied to the mission, are ethically transparent and accountable, generate income through trade, and the mission is locked for any transfer of ownership.

See the Terms to Know (page xxi) for more explanations of terms related to social enterprise.

positive impact in order to be considered a social enterprise? How should the business measure its impact—in dollars raised, in lives saved, in people employed, in trees planted? Who gets to decide what levels or degrees of impact qualifies a business to be labeled as a social enterprise? Does donating money to a cause under the umbrella of corporate responsibility give a company license to call itself a social enterprise?

These questions are not easily answered, which is why it's difficult to have a crystal clear definition of the term. In fact, although the above organizations have come up with their own definitions, "social enterprise" doesn't even exist in Merriam-Webster's dictionary as of 2022. Part of the reason is that it's still a relatively new concept, which has only grown in popularity over the past decade.

Of course, there are a few social enterprises that have been around for a while now. Goodwill Industries, for example, was founded in 1902 with the idea of giving the poor "a hand up, not a hand out" by employing them to repair goods that could then be resold to the general public. Although the organization is legally registered as a 501(c)(3) nonprofit, it is largely funded by its large network of retail thrift stores, which provide work for underprivileged and second-chance workers, while also increasing the circularity of clothing and home goods to promote sustainability. As a representative for the San Francisco chain of Goodwill stores explained, "As a unique hybrid called a social enterprise, we defy traditional distinctions. Instead of a single bottom line of profit, we hold ourselves accountable to a triple bottom line of people, planet, and performance."

Then there are companies like Patagonia, which is a for-profit business founded in 1973. The company is well known not only for its high-quality outdoor apparel and gear, but also for its social and environmental responsibility. Yvon Chouinard founded Patagonia on four main values: quality, integrity, environmentalism, and innovation. As he and his team have remained true to those values over the past fifty years, they have truly become a leader in sustainability and transparency, setting an example for other social enterprises to follow.

Organizations like Goodwill and Patagonia, however, have been the exception, not the norm. For the most part, the idea that an organization could make a profit while also doing good in the world is a trend that's only recently gained significant momentum. In the past decade, universities around the world have introduced Social Entrepreneurship programs and career tracks. In 2015, *Forbes* magazine began releasing a yearly list of 30 Under 30 Social Entrepreneurs to complement their popular 30 Under 30 list of the most successful young "conventional" entrepreneurs.

The ideals and principles of social enterprise are still just beginning and starting to gain significant traction. New businesses that are built on social impact initiatives are forming everyday. For some, the product or service they are providing has direct impact with specific causes or social initiatives. For others, they are more traditional businesses that are engaging in social impact and becoming social enterprises. Carpenters, plumbers, manufacturers, retail and grocery resellers, and restauranteurs are also thinking about ways they can have a social impact. Ideas like second-chance employment, workforce development, using clean or natural raw materials, and profit-sharing are all concepts that are being incorporated into businesses today. I truly believe that every business can be on the journey of social entrepreneurship, and it is through our collective impact that we can solve our greatest social challenges.

Section 2

There's No Such Thing as a Perfect Business

As entrepreneurs and business leaders, we're trying to "do good" inside of a broken system that makes "good" very difficult to achieve. We have been living in our current capitalist system for several generations at this point. All the good and bad that go with it are ingrained in our thinking. As we begin the journey of using the tools of business to positively impact our world, we have to keep in mind that it is not easy to try to change how we operate on a day-to-day basis. And as we've discussed, good is incredibly difficult if not impossible to quantify and measure. While we wrestle with the definition of good, I have found that for many social entrepreneurs, good can sometimes feel like it's never good enough.

Perhaps it isn't.

But, what if that's OK?

Often we can get caught up in the concepts of good versus perfect. I've sometimes witnessed perfectionism stall any progress at all. "If it can't be perfect, then what's the point?" I'm not sure perfect is achievable in any aspect of life—let alone social enterprise. There will always be something we can all do just a little better to deepen our impact. I think it's healthy to acknowledge that, but we should also not let it paralyze and stop us. It reminds me of a slogan by the auto manufacturer Lexus from a few years ago: "The Relentless Pursuit of

Perfection." Striving for perfection should encourage us to keep moving forward, and in our pursuit, we continue to learn and see new possibilities. I would assume that Lexus's definition of perfection was about the performance, safety, and comfort of their vehicles. Imagine if the idea of perfection also started to include better sourcing practices and greener emissions. Good is something that can keep getting better and better.

We could continue going around and around talking about what qualifications an organization must hold in order to qualify as having a "positive impact." We could go back and forth discussing who's "in" and who's "out" of the social enterprise club. We could argue about which certifications are more reliable or effective, and which type of business structure is best suited to solve our social ills. We could have endless debates about the pros and cons of early capitalism, hyper-capitalism, socialism, and the like.

I don't want to argue against wrestling with these questions, but we need to enter these debates with caution. First, we need to guard our energies in these conversations. They take work, can tap into deep emotions, and can continue with no end in sight. If we are not careful, they can distract us from actually doing the work that we are passionate about doing.

Second, we need to recognize that perfect is often the enemy of good. There can be a danger of paralysis in these debates—that if we can't do all that we set out to do, then we don't do anything. We cannot let the expectation of perfection and the inability to do everything we want at this moment stop us from the good we can do today and at this moment.

Section 3

Every Business Can Be a Good Business

For the purposes of this book, I'd like to view social enterprise as a spectrum, as opposed to a concrete set of criteria. My goal is to encourage and empower any and all businesses to start making a positive impact today, no matter where they currently stand on the spectrum of "good." I believe that when you boil it down to its simplest form, every business can be a social enterprise. There are no "good" or "bad," "positive" or "negative" organizations; there are only those that are farther along on the scale of impact. That means that no matter what your business's model is today, or what labels you have or have not put on it, you can start making a beneficial change right now.

For many, this may require a bit of a mindset shift—a change in the fundamental way you approach your work or business. It entails a transition away from box-checking and toward a focus on the overall journey. It becomes more about how you're approaching your business and its purpose on a fundamental level, as opposed to just what you're doing.

Let's look at it this way: Pretend it's possible to create an objective "responsibility" or "impact" scale, from zero to one hundred. A score of zero indicates the least responsible, least ethical company out there that's doing absolutely nothing good for anyone. A score of one hundred means the company is doing everything perfectly in every area. The company with a perfect one hundred score* would be creating a high-quality product that customers need at a fair price while benefiting their workers and communities and not exploiting the environment. Their overall "net" impact would be positive, and there would be no room left for improvement throughout their entire operation.

Let's say you own or work for a business that has a strong social purpose and does a lot of good in the world—maybe your company sits somewhere near the seventy-five mark. But, what if your business isn't really doing much good at all, sitting somewhere around a five on our spectrum? You have just as much, if not more opportunity to create an incredible amount of positive change.

As an example, let's imagine an organic cotton clothing company. The brand's textiles hold several third-party organic certifications, which ensure that no harmful herbicides or pesticides were used to grow the cotton, and that the farmers were paid a fair wage for their crop. Let's give this brand a hypothetical score of eighty. It is doing really great work to move the industry toward a more sustainable future. But, what's the next step the company's team can take? Perhaps they go beyond organic and work toward transitioning their textiles to regenerative cotton. Not only does regenerative cotton "do no harm" by excluding toxic chemicals, but it actually restores and heals the soil in the way that it's grown and harvested. Switching from organic to regenerative textiles might move this company's "score" up to an eighty-five.

Alternatively, let's imagine a clothing company that's much lower on the spectrum than the previous example. This brand uses only virgin synthetics in its textiles. These materials

---

* This company with a perfect score is a hypothetical one; I personally believe that no such organization exists at this time.

are petroleum-based, require harmful chemicals to produce (chemicals which leach out into waterways and harm garment workers in the process), and will not biodegrade at the end of their life. Perhaps this brand's "score" is only a five, but the company takes a step in the right direction and transitions 50 percent of its fabrics to ECONYL®, a textile made from recycled plastic bottles. The "score" goes up, and the next year the brand adds even more recycled and natural materials into its products. The year after that, it moves production to Fair Trade Certified factories. The company slowly and steadily makes progress, inching up the scale in a way that allows it to increase its positive impact while also growing a financially sustainable business.

The point is that every business can be on the journey toward "social enterprise" if its fundamental goal of operation is to steadily move up on the spectrum. Every organization can take at least one baby step each and every day to move its needle closer to 100. No one is left out of making our world a better place, which is pretty fun to think about.

To take it a step further, it might be helpful to view our hypothetical spectrum in two different ways: holistically, or broken down into the different areas of business. Let's use La Terza Coffee as an example. La Terza pays all its farmers a fair wage for their product, so it should score relatively well when thinking about social procurement or the "supply chain scale"—let's say it gets an eighty. La Terza would probably score lower, however, on the "environment scale." Some of our coffee is certified organic, but not all of it. Additionally, although we do compost our coffee grounds, not all our packaging is recycled or biodegradable, and we could afford to decrease the amount of overall waste generated by our production. Therefore, we might score a forty-five on the Environmental Scale. If we were to come up with a score for each of our identified categories and then average all our scores together, we might come up with an overall score of seventy. We're doing well and moving in the right direction, but there is always room for progress. Breaking the scores down in this way can help business leaders, managers, and employees gain clarity on which categories hold the most room for improvement, which areas will be prioritized during a certain time frame, and how the company is doing as a whole.

While scores can help us to measure and quantify our impact, it's also important to remember that the point is not the number. All of these scores are hypothetical and they are ultimately not about checking boxes or earning a good score for moral bragging rights. Rather, they are about implementing long-term, holistic approaches to your work, and taking small, intentional, and effective steps in a certain direction in order to build a business that's sustainable for people, planet, and profit.

Section 4

Corporate Social Responsibility

At this point, I've written a lot about what I think social enterprise is, and not so much about what it isn't. That's intentional. As we've just talked about, I truly believe that every business can be a part of making the world a better place.

I grew up and live in Cincinnati, Ohio, which is home to two of the largest corporations in the world: Kroger, and Proctor and Gamble. According to the National Retail Federation, in 2022 Kroger is the fifth largest retailer in the world, behind Walmart, Amazon, Costco, and The Home Depot with over 3,000 grocery stores. Proctor and Gamble, whose history began with producing soap, is a multinational consumer goods company that generated over $76 billion in revenue in 2021.

I would argue that building grocery stores is a way to help farmers and food producers bring food to communities, and that is socially a good thing to do. I would also make an uncontested argument that soap is necessary for cleanliness, and making products that enable us to stay healthy is important. Providing access to food and cleaning products is fundamentally a social need. I am not here to say that because there is a baseline of good in the business models of Kroger, Proctor and Gamble, and other corporations, it makes them social enterprises. But with that being said, I really struggle to say that these companies and the roots of their organizations are not engaged in some positive way, even if it's minimal.

We also have to recognize that corporations are taking steps to make positive changes. Corporate social responsibility is a trending type of business self-regulation with the aim of becoming more socially accountable. With the number of socially conscious consumers growing, more and more employees and customers are placing a premium on working for and spending their money with businesses that prioritize CSR. Of course, there are also many negative stories within the history of Kroger and Proctor and Gamble, and plenty has been written about wrongs they have committed. Many arguments have also been made that CSR initiatives overall are designed to offset and distract from a company's negative impact. This might be true, but when looking objectively at both Kroger and Proctor and Gamble, I think there is a need to recognize that some amazing initiatives that have been started and they are having a tremendous positive social impact.

In 2018, Kroger established the Zero Hunger | Zero Waste Foundation as a nonprofit public charity designed to create a more equitable food system. The dream is that everyone has access to affordable, nutritious food and no surplus food is wasted, and the foundation is partnering with supporting organizations and innovators across the country who share the same passion. The United States discards nearly 40 million tons of food every year—more than any other country, which is estimated to be 30–40 percent of the entire US food supply. In fact, food is the single largest component taking up space in US landfills. Meanwhile, prior to the COVID-19 pandemic, it was estimated that 35 million people across America suffered from food insecurity, including 10 million children. That number is expected to increase in 2022 as we are still working through effects of the pandemic, our supply chains issues, inflation, employment drops, and other financial-related issues.

Clearly there is a gap we need to address because we are producing enough food where no one should be hungry. No one else is in a better position to solve such a large problem. And we need companies like Kroger to help us bridge this gap. Collectively, we can celebrate them and work with them to find real solutions.

Because Kroger and Proctor and Gamble are two of Cincinnati's largest employers and Cincinnati is a relatively small city, I personally know quite a few people who work for each company. I can assure you that some of the smartest, kindest, most caring individuals work at these organizations. They believe in meaningful work and playing their part in making deep social impact. From my perspective, they have amazing opportunities to engage with social causes through their work. They are stepping up, leading initiatives, and having an influence on shaping the companies they work for as they begin to make positive changes from within.

Let's Start with What's Good

As I mentioned earlier, I worked for Wendy's when I was in college. I loved my time working there, and I think there are many ways that Wendy's engages in local communities. For me, this was just a normal part-time job and I was fortunate enough to work with a fantastic team—many whom were also in college—that took a lot of pride in their work. We loved the challenge of serving quality food, while also working very quickly. Because of this team culture, we were recognized as a training store and many managers came through while learning Wendy's systems of management and leadership. For managers in training, Wendy's offered assistance in helping people finish GED programs while also helping people find a potential long-term career path, and while also being paid enough to achieve financial stability. This is a social idea.

Wendy's was founded by Dave Thomas, and part of his story is that he was adopted as an infant. Dave began working in fast food at the young age of twelve, and through innovation, hard work, a passion for quality control, and great marketing campaigns he built Wendy's into the third largest hamburger chain in the world. With a personal connection to adoption, Dave realized how a stable home life could lift someone into a better story. Sadly, more than twenty thousand children aged out of the foster care system in 2021, leaving them at a higher risk for homelessness, unemployment, and many other negative outcomes. In 1992, with Dave's story and personal success as the founder of Wendy's, he launched the Dave Thomas Foundation for Adoption with the core belief that "no child should linger in foster care or leave the system without a permanent family." Today, through its signature program "Wendy's Wonderful Kids," the foundation enables adoption professionals to find loving, permanent homes for children who are waiting in foster care. This, too, is a social idea.

I am not arguing that these ideas make Wendy's a social enterprise. But I am here to say that these are just two ways that Wendy's has initiated long-standing, positive impacts in our society.

I dream of one day talking to the CEO of Wendy's about the foundational principles of social enterprise. Imagine in that meeting, I begin by listing all of Wendy's shortcomings as a business and community citizen. Then I cast a vision about how Wendy's, with a couple of shifts in perspective, could launch some significant social initiatives and programs benefiting new segments of our society. When I imagine that scenario, I quickly see myself being escorted from the building.

But imagine this. . . . I begin with all the ways I see Wendy's having a positive impact: using their business to help managers pursue higher education and continuing their support of the Dave Thomas Foundation for Adoption. At that point, we talk about other ways that Wendy's could have a social impact. My guess is that there would be at least an opportunity to continue the dialogue.

One of the most challenged segments of society are those who have been incarcerated and are looking for long-term, living-wage employment. Many people with prison records, who have paid their debts to society and are trying to find a new path, are often shut out from finding healthy and stable employment.

Drawing from my experience of how Wendy's empowered managers, both through their training programs and through educational support, I think that Wendy's is in a prime position to create radical opportunities for many Americans pursuing a positive path forward. And just as Kroger is in one of the best positions to tackle the issues of food insecurity and food waste, I believe that Wendy's is in a prime position to become radical and transform the way we treat people who need a second chance. Can you see it?

This idea also reinforces the importance of viewing social enterprise as a journey and that all of us can join the movement. We talked about how I scored La Terza and our social impact, and if I were to average all of our scores, I would grade us as maybe a seventy overall. I have so many ideas about where I want to lead to, but I can actually become overwhelmed by how much work is still needed to maximize our impact on our journey to one hundred. The weight of this feeling has a negative effect when I put too much thought into it. I can find myself focusing on all the things we aren't doing yet and how much energy and resources are required to get to that level, rather than keeping my attention on what we are doing currently and what could be accomplished next. It becomes disheartening and I don't want to pursue the next steps. But, when I stay focused on only the next few steps, I pull myself back into feelings of hope.

So, when I imagine an opportunity to dream about social impact with the CEO of Wendy's, I am aware that they will likely have a similar mindset. They will not be interested in learning how to be the best at social enterprise, a "one hundred." I doubt they'd even be interested in being like La Terza at seventy. But, what if one shift in thinking could help them move from where they are today, a one or two, to a five or six? And if they seriously considered launching a second-chance employment program, maybe they could become a ten.

For Wendy's to follow my scenario, we have to begin with what is good. There are great things that Wendy's is engaged with, and with a few new perspectives, they could play a significant role in transforming so many more people's lives. Second, by sheer scale, if Wendy's did move from a two to a five —or even a three!—the scale of their impact would dwarf the impact of La Terza moving from a seventy to one hundred. This would be such a beautiful story; it makes me smile to dream of the possibility of it. It also makes me feel a little of what I believe we all need right now, a tangible and real sense of hope.

Section 5

Give-Back Models

Another model that we have seen emerge and gain momentum over the past decade is the idea of giving back. Popularized by TOMS' clear message to "Buy One, Give One," it's become popular among small- and medium-size brands that are at the beginning of their social impact journey. With every purchase, the brand gives back a product to someone in need. For every backpack sold, they might give a backpack to a child living in poverty in the US. Or for every pair of glasses sold, they might donate a pair to someone who is visually impaired and doesn't have access to an eye doctor.

These can be great models to follow, and the message to the consumer is very clear. These organizations can also have significant impact that is easily measurable. For example, I love the certification "1% for the Planet." When I see their logo and certification on packages of the products I purchase, I know exactly how a company is having an impact in tackling our planet's most pressing environmental issues.

This model is something to celebrate, but I also want to keep encouraging the idea of social enterprise in ways that are holistic throughout the entire organization. Let's keep asking how products are sourced, how they might affect a local economy, and where they are made. We should acknowledge the idea that "teaching people to fish" is better than "giving a fish." When people are hungry and don't know where their next meal will come from, we absolutely should be giving fish! But also, let's keep going and give them opportunities and resources to move beyond an unhealthy dependency. Asking hard questions around how products given in these programs could potentially do more harm than good is worthwhile and healthy.

The idea of giving back is pure in heart and intention. The message is clear: the consumer is a partner and directly engaged with the cause, and it is a fantastic first step toward social impact. If this is something you are thinking about including in your business model, please do! The more people that join the radical party of social enterprise, the more we can learn from and support one another. Let's also keep the party going, looking for the next steps of the journey in using the tools of business to make the world a better place.

Section 6

Minding All Stakeholders

There is one last important relationship to consider when it comes to how you run your social impact business: investors. Not all businesses, especially small ones, have them. However, as any business scales, opportunities could arise to bring in investment resources. Bringing on investors can often be a really good thing. It means your business has the potential to grow, and investors also are often motivated to help beyond bringing monetary resources. But with every investment, there is the question of "what is the return on the investment (ROI)?" Whether time, money, or skills are being invested, the investor will want to know what their reward will be.

For any business, taking time to get to know and trust your investment team is critical. Going through all the details can be a long process, but it's very important to make sure that everyone's goals are talked through and aligned. For social impact businesses, taking the time to be clear about these goals and expectations with investors is even more critical to define, as often the ROI might not always be about the income generated.

It's always at least a little bit risky for both the investors as well as the business and its leadership. Investors are taking a financial risk, while owners and CEOs risk having to compromise the business's foundational values in order to keep investors happy. Ideally, your investors will be personally and/or professionally passionate about the causes with which your business is involved. Short-term ROI and long-term financial success are both important, so make sure everyone is clear on the business's priorities, and under which circumstances immediate financial return might be sacrificed in order to make the best decision. It's also important that your investor knows that he or she is not the only stakeholder in the business, and that the company's leadership will be considering all other stakeholders as well.

Bringing on investors can also be an opportunity. Not only could they be needed in order to start a new social enterprise —in both financial contribution and expertise—but maybe they could be learning about how business can have significant positive impacts. As we continue to read together, you'll learn there are several arguments to be made that social enterprises can be more profitable for organizations. So, the opportunity to invite others into social enterprise can be a really great thing, too. Just make sure you take the needed time to be fully on the same page, both in conversations and in writing.

One of the best ways to move toward common alignment is to work together on defining a company's values. Decisions on many different issues arise regularly in any business, and there's often more than one way to solve problems. Values can be a guide, both on how a business runs on a daily basis as well as when a tough problem needs to be solved. And when values are written down and agreed upon before the work begins, they also can be a great reference point as disagreements arise.

While there is caution to consider in adding investors, partners, and other stakeholders, I do want to say it can also be deeply rewarding to invite others into the journey. I like to use an analogy that adding investors is a lot like a romantic relationship. You want to take time to "date" and really get to know each other. Small projects, meetings, and dreaming of future goals all help to establish trust. Eventually, you see a green light to take a leap of faith, move forward, and commit to a long-term relationship. And just like our personal relationships going to the next level, partnerships in our work can be among life's most rewarding and beautiful experiences.

Section 7

You May Say I'm a Dreamer, but I'm Not the Only One

You have probably realized by now that I am an idealist. Although the world does not exist in black and white, in some areas of life I find myself wishing it did. I wish that we celebrated our black-and-white differences and the messy middle gray space between us was viewed as a sacred space of bringing in different perspectives and learning from one another. I also see the truths that are not in the middle. For example, if love and hate are two ends of a spectrum, the middle view of tolerance is not what we should be aiming for. How do we keep striving toward truly loving one another regardless of race, religion, culture, gender, or sexual orientation? Coming together with postures of curiosity, humility, and giving others the benefit of the doubt when we feel wronged would go a long way toward becoming a better version of humanity.

I have to constantly fight against seeing the world in terms of good and bad instead leaving room for the complicated and realistic nuance that exists in almost everything. As difficult as this internal conflict might be, I also maintain that at the heart of my idealism lies a seed for great potential. It is this mindset that leads me to hope that every business big and small can do good. Of course, there are people who are primarily driven by profit at any cost, but I also believe that most people are good and want to help make the world a better place. Reimagining a new, equitable economy is no longer a dream that is out of reach. It is a present reality that is within our grasp.

So, in acknowledging that social enterprise is hard to define, in recognizing that there is no such thing as perfect and that all businesses can work toward having a positive social impact, I will be using the term "social enterprise" liberally in the coming sections. You can read social enterprise as "a business that is on a path to decreasing its negative impact and increasing its positive impact." That business might be taking its very first step, or it may have been making strides for decades. Either way, it is slowly and steadily making progress up our hypothetical scale. Social enterprises are in a constant and continual state of progress. They are always identifying the next step to take, tackling the next problem, and working toward the next solution.

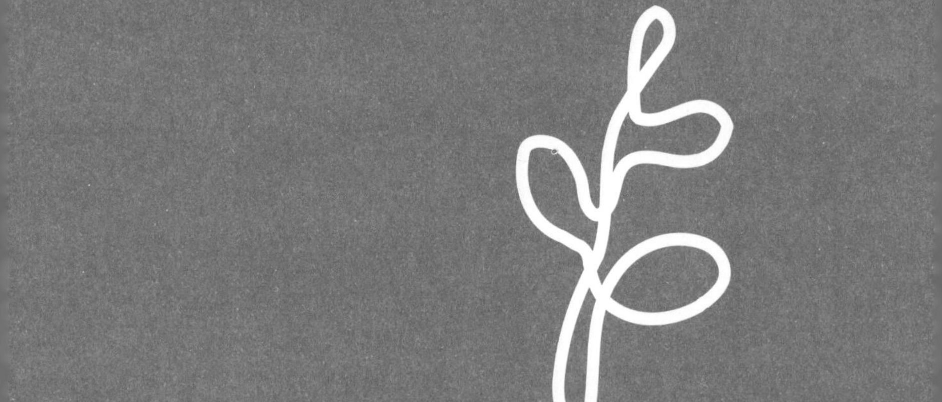

PART 2

The Seven Seeds

So, what does a radical business look like in the next decade? As we enter into an era of a new economy, I'm curious to learn the answers to some new questions. What does it mean to go back to the roots of business and provide value in a world where hyper-capitalism, climate change, and inequality have gotten out of control? If businesses are set up to solve consumer problems, how might we actually use that same set of tools to solve other problems too, such as modern-day slavery, poverty, and hunger?

As I have wrestled with the idea of business going back to the basics, I'm reminded that businesses are really about people. They're made up of people, exchanging goods and services among ourselves, literally so we can live and bring life to one another. Food, shelter, medical supplies, clothing, shipping, transportation, and education are all areas of products and services that we provide for others through our work. We are inherently interdependent because not one of us has all of the skills needed to be completely self-sufficient. We need each other, and that's a radical, root idea that we need to return to.

In thinking about our interconnected humanity, I'm also reminded of part of my earliest learning, the Golden Rule: Treat other people the way you want to be treated. I can visualize this poster hanging in my elementary school classes and how it was the foundation of classroom etiquette. Rules like keep your hands to yourself, take turns, and raise your hand are all a part of how we interact with others.

So, when I think about business going back to its original purpose—that business is about people—and I marry that with the principles of the Golden Rule, it helps me think about that definition of social enterprise again. Maybe a radical business simply treats other people and businesses the way they would want to be treated. And if that's the base principle, it then leads me to ask, "Who does a business interact with?"

Over the years, my role in the small business and social enterprise community has expanded beyond CEO of La Terza. I've served as board chairperson of the Social Enterprise Alliance, as a speaker for various positive impact groups, and as a cohost for both the Third Place podcast and Social Enterprise Alliance podcast, the latter of which centers around the themes of positive-impact businesses. Through all of this work, that question of "who" has remained with me, and I've been actively trying to identify all of the people-groups businesses engage with. It is this question that led me to see there are seven groups of people that every business touches.

I also really like the idea of calling the following seven areas "seeds." Each of these areas, once identified, helped me to understand how La Terza could create new paths of impact. They also helped give me a way to measure, and to recognize that we were nowhere near the level of impact we wanted to have. In some ways, this was actually discouraging. But as we've discussed, when you just look at the next step—not where you want to end up, but what you can do next ——you begin to see the path as a long journey.

The lens of these Seven Seeds has helped me to see that when small business owners or managers take small, actionable, and accessible steps toward making a positive impact in each of these categories, radical things unfold. We all have an opportunity to make a direct and positive impact in the world simply by operating our business with a small shift in our thinking. We also set ourselves up for long-term, profitable success while welcoming into the fold new generations of leaders and consumers.

Small steps toward social impact are ideas that are ready to be planted. They are like coffee trees, which take five years to mature before they bear fruit that can be harvested to yield a good crop. It's a commitment. But when it does bear fruit, when the plant has been properly cared for, pruned, and nurtured, the fruit is worth the wait.

Plant, Water, Grow

When I dream of the world with a brand-new evolving economy, I imagine a large, sturdy oak tree that has taken a generation to grow and mature. It's so easy to forget that a magnificent tree could start as small seed, but that's how it works!

A new economy is on its way. So, if radical means "root" or "origin," and seeds are the beginnings of large plants and trees, it makes me feel like we're planting a garden. Seeds have been planted. Many more seeds continue to be planted and cared for today. Even more seeds still need to be planted in each of the seven areas of impact. These Seven Seeds are future trees that will grow and provide new foundations for businesses, people, and the planet.

As we dive deeper into each of the seven seeds, my hope is that we all can walk away with practical ways to begin this journey. At the end of each segment, we will talk through how we can "plant, water, and grow" these seeds: learning how to incorporate shifts in our mindsets, actively looking for micro-opportunities and begin new ways to have impact, and fully integrating growth and traction with each group.

Plant: Taking steps to shift our mindset and perspectives

Water: Actively looking for micro-opportunities to begin new ways to have impact

Grow: How to fully integrate and build traction

There is power in all of us doing this together, and if all of us begin to take small steps we will be able to see significant impact. Remember, we are all ants, and we are a powerful force when we unite. We are holding seeds that could one day be a forest. It's time to go and get our hands dirty as we learn how to plant, water, and grow each seed together.

Seed 1

Supply Chain
Behind Every Product Is a Story

Before I began working with La Terza, I was completely unaware of the incredible injustices in the larger coffee industry. There are 12.5 million coffee farms, and 12.4 million are smallholders who produce close to 80 percent of the world's coffee. More than 50 percent live in poverty, all while working extremely long hours in the sun and being constantly exposed to herbicides and pesticides that are known to cause cancer and other serious health issues. Because they're not paid a reasonable fair wage for their work, the majority of farmers and their workers simply aren't able to make ends meet. To make matters worse, they are still expected to meet quotas even when coffee prices decline, meaning that during certain years, they get even less money for the same amount of work. Because of this, many families are forced to pull their young children out of school to help, so child labor runs rampant in the industry.

It's worth noting that the majority of coffee-growing countries are considered "developing." More economically prosperous regions like the United States—with the exception of Hawaii—Europe, and Australia don't have the climates that are conducive for growing coffee. Instead, almost all of the coffee we drink is grown in what some call the "Bean Belt," which runs along the equator and includes countries like Mexico, Brazil, and Ethiopia. This is worth noting because many of the countries where coffee is grown and harvested also happen to be places with widespread poverty and systems of deep injustice. Because of this, most coffee farmers and farmworkers are, in a sense, stuck between a rock and a hard place. They do not have many other options for work, they do not have negotiating power, and they are at the mercy of the company paying them. They essentially have no choice but to take what they are given even if it means accepting payment that's far below the living wage they deserve.

Unfortunately, the injustice doesn't stop there. There are countless other men, women, and children who are not just severely underpaid and overworked, but in fact truly enslaved on coffee plantations. Also called bonded labor or debt peonage, workers are manipulated into accepting a "job"— often in a country that's not their home—and then are trapped, physically unable to leave, and more often than not, abused. Many times, farm owners, brokers, or other middlemen pay a portion of the fees "required" for the worker to emigrate, leaving the workers indebted to them. These fees are usually charged by the employer and are to some extent fabricated. Then, once the workers get to their new destination, they're either not paid what they were promised, the interest on the "loans" they were given to travel outweigh their salaries, or both. It is impossible for them to pay off their debt and become free workers; therefore, they are trapped in bonded labor. Sadly, this type of slavery is all too common today.

As an example, take a 2011 case between the US Equal Employment Opportunity Commission (EEOC) and eight different farms in Hawaii and Washington State. The EEOC filed a human trafficking lawsuit against the farms after discovering they were forcing hundreds of Thai men to work against their will. These men had been legally brought to the US under a visa program and they paid exorbitant fees to their brokers and employers to emigrate. Lacking work opportunities at home, they were promised jobs and fair salaries in the United States. As the lawsuit investigation revealed, when the Thai workers arrived at the farms, their employers confiscated their passports to prevent them from leaving. The men were constantly threatened with deportation, physically assaulted by supervisors, and starved while living in cramped and guarded facilities. At least two of the eight farms involved in the lawsuit were coffee plantations, while the others were fruit farms. It's a stark reality that bonded labor occurs not only in the coffee industry but also in food agriculture, the garment industry, mining, and other sectors.

Notice that this specific example involves farms in the United States, where there are laws, regulations, investigative journalists, and other systems in place that are meant to hold companies accountable for these inhumane actions. The problem, however, is that in most of the regions of the world where coffee is grown, there is no EEOC investigating wrongdoing or working to bring freedom and justice to victims. Many of the corrupt or ill-equipped governments of the Bean Belt countries are either involved in the injustice, turn a blind eye to it for various reasons, or simply don't have the resources to do anything about it.

Even though there's been a hopeful uptick in the amount of coffee that's ethically traded in the past decade, most coffee companies still overlook the true origins of their beans. They buy their product from third-party middlemen and have virtually no information about what occurred from the time it was planted until it got to their roasterie or shop. Coffee-loving consumers are none the wiser about the fact that their favorite beverage could be fueling not only their work days but also a brutal slave trade.

La Terza was different. I loved La Terza's concept from the start, but as I got to know its business model more deeply, my eyes were opened to the possibility of just how much good a for-profit business could do. From the very beginning, ethical sourcing was the foundation on which La Terza was built. After all, how could you create the best cup of coffee possible using beans picked by someone trapped in bonded labor?

My "Aha" Moment

In 2018, five years after I began working in coffee, I took my first trip to a coffee plantation. Our primary direct-trade coffee relationship is with a woman producer, Katia Duke in Honduras. We often get many samples of coffee sent our way, but when we tasted her coffee, it made quite the impression on our team for how good it tasted. Little did we know that Katia was also using her profits to build a school for her community and had begun the plans to build a large kitchen next to the school so that the kids could be provided a daily and nutritious meal. Her coffee plantation was a living and breathing example of a social enterprise.

During the trip, there was one moment that stuck out more than any other. We had just finished a tour of the gorgeous plantation and I was introduced to a team of women sorting out the coffee beans by hand.

One of the older women sorting the beans was doing her job with so much joy. She was humming along as she worked, and she had a huge smile on her face the entire time we were there. I was happy to know that through our relationship with Katia, this woman was being paid properly. But what struck me the most was how happy this woman was. As I left that space, I remember saying out loud to myself, "This is why we need to keep working hard to roast every batch of coffee to perfection." Of course, being able to provide living wages is a huge part of social enterprise, but this woman reminded me that it's also so much deeper. Joy is important.

SPECIALTY COFFEE ROASTER

Even with the best care and farming practices, not all coffee grown ends up going to roasters like La Terza! We are known as a "specialty coffee roaster," meaning we only serve the best of the best. Once the coffee is harvested—which is itself a process of hand-selection—it goes through one final inspection where the largest, most mature, and defect-free coffee beans are separated from the rest. Coffee that does not pass this test is set aside for commodity-grade coffee (think large restaurant chains), or processed as instant coffee.

Even in the menial tasks, we can be happy with our work. To be human is to work and create. When we do not pay appropriately for things produced around the world, like coffee, it's more than the monetary transaction. It's about robbing someone of their human existence and identity. We are connected to this woman and everyone who drinks our coffee is, too. And the work of her hands matters.

Can you remember the first thing you made and sold with your own two hands? Maybe it was your first lemonade stand, or a puppet show to which you sold tickets. Or it could have been the first day at an after-school job. Sure, it may have been a small, ordinary moment. The money you earned might have come from patronizing family members or neighbors who wanted to support you more than they really wanted your product. These experiences are significant to our young minds. They can be instrumental in how we develop our view of work, and how we learn to value human creation.

How often do you think about the hands that make the goods you use? It takes a conscious effort to think about who picks the tomatoes you buy from the grocery store, and who sews the hems on your T-shirts. If you're like I was, you never even thought to ask your barista about the farmers who harvested the espresso in your latte.

It didn't take long after I began working with La Terza to discover how corrupt a coffee company's supply chain could be. Most coffee companies both large and small work with third party importers to source their beans. The coffee roaster—usually headquartered in a high-coffee-consuming country in Europe or North America—works with a middle-man company that coordinates with coffee farmers to source green, unroasted beans. Because of this, most coffee roasteries and shops have very little information about the region or country where the beans are grown. Today, more coffee shops and roasteries are learning to care more about that information, and the interest of consumers is driving some changes. These businesses are passionate about serving great coffee and they want to share great stories. But coffee is consumed in many places that do not share the passion of serving great coffee and knowing where it comes from. Restaurants, offices, hotels, gas stations, hospitals are all examples of places that consume a lot of coffee but likely couldn't tell you anything about where the coffee is from, the actual coffee farmer, the conditions under which the farmer's team are working, how much they're being paid for the product, whether there were any children doing the work, or what their lives are like.

One of the driving forces of the local food movement is the idea of knowing the story behind what we consume. By focusing on purchasing more in our regions, we are closer to people in our communities. More money stays in our local economies, less shipping is required, seasonality is celebrated, and we are more aware of the healthy interdependence of our humanity.

The idea of buying local, of course, is not new. Before the Industrial Revolution in the late eighteenth century, followed by globalization beginning in the 1820s, most people were familiar with where their goods came from and who was making or growing them. Your furniture was likely carved and assembled by a nearby carpenter out of locally sourced wood. Your shoes came from the cobbler down the street. Your clothes might have been made by your mother, and the yarn she used was probably spun by local farmers out of wool from their flocks. You may have gotten most of your food from that same farmer. In this localized economy, you were more naturally in tune with the impact of your purchasing decisions. You were more aware of whether your purchase was a fair transaction for both parties. You could look your farmer, your shoemaker, your seamstress, or your carpenter in the eye and have real conversations. Prior to globalization, nearly all supply chains were significantly simpler, more localized, and more transparent than they are today.

Of course, global trade has nearly always been a part of human history. Raw materials and products like tea, grains, and metals have been traded for many centuries. Unfortunately, knowing the producers of these raw materials was not really possible. And if it was, the dark side of poor working conditions and human slavery was not brought to light.

When you fast-forward to the twenty-first century, a primary change is that we have many more finished products available that have been made in other parts of the world. Generally in the past, raw materials from global sources were brought to local crafters who made the final products. As transportation evolved with better ships, railroads, and airplanes, the cost of moving goods from one place to the next continued to go down. Eventually, with lower labor costs in other parts of the world and the lower costs to move items, it made financial sense to have final products produced across the globe. So many of our basic needs like clothing, computers, cars, and books are made overseas. It is true that different countries have different economies and the value of the dollar varies drastically; a living wage in another country could be as little as seven US dollars today. Unfortunately, most of us are not aware that lower costs are often associated with poor living and working conditions. Consumers and businesses are only beginning to ask better questions about who is making their goods and where or how the materials used to make those goods are sourced.

Coffee is not the only industry with problems. Corruption and unethical practices exist in supply chains across many sectors. You've probably heard about dangerous garment sweatshops, the blood diamonds that fuel violence and war, and child labor in the fishing industry. Meat packers and producers along with fruit farmworkers also easily find themselves trapped in bonded slavery. Complexity leads to a lack of transparency, contributing to the unethical practices that run rampant throughout our globalized supply chains.

It's important to note here that a "transparent," "simple," or "local" supply chain does not automatically mean that it's an ethical one. Unjust supply chains can be found throughout human history, especially with the introduction of agriculture about eleven thousand years ago. In seventeenth- and eighteenth-century America, of course, certain products and services—tobacco, cane sugar, cotton, rice, and carpentry—were often harvested and built by the hands of the enslaved. This was a transparent and simple supply chain, but by no means an ethical one. The complex and murky nature of today's globalized supply chains is a critical factor fueling our current injustices. As social entrepreneurs, we cannot move forward to ensure ethical and humane production without first untangling these sinuous supply chains and insisting on radical transparency.

The Simplicity and Complexity of Supply Chains

For a business and its complete supply chain, coffee is relatively simple. We purchase green coffee from farmers and importers, it is shipped to us, we roast it, and then distribute it to our customers. Of course, there are many other small pieces to the business of roasting coffee, from office supplies, boxes, and packaging to items like office furniture, computers, company shirts, mugs, and coffee-brewing equipment.

A simple supply chain looks something like this:

And a typical coffee supply chain looks like this:

In comparison, something like an electronic device requires many more components. Take a cell phone, for example. Instead of just one raw ingredient like green coffee beans, you need:

- **Glass**, which is made of things like aluminum oxide and silicon dioxide
- **Aluminum alloys**, which are lightweight metals commonly found in a phone's case

- **Lithium cobalt oxide and carbon graphite** to make the battery
- **Other metals** like gold, copper, platinum, tungsten, and silver for the wiring of the phone
- **Still other metals** like neodymium-iron-boron alloys, dysprosium, and praseodymium, which are used to make the speakers
- **Plastics** for frames, buttons, and casings (made from raw materials like crude oil)

There are individuals and companies—often located in completely different parts of the world—involved in the extraction and manufacturing of every single one of those ingredients. And this is just to create the hardware of the actual device—we haven't even mentioned the other ingredients, processes, and parties involved. Think about the software designers, transportation companies, third-party auditors and inspectors, government regulators, packaging manufacturers, retail store workers, and more. Here is a still somewhat simplified example of an electronic device supply chain:

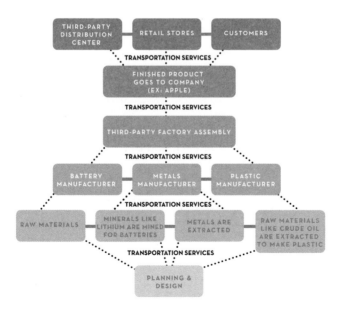

Another example would be for a piece of apparel. It's not as complicated as an electronics supply chain, but it might be more complex than you think. A variety of raw materials are needed: natural plant-based fibers like cotton and linen, animal-based materials like wool, leather, and cashmere, and synthetic fibers like polyester and spandex. Other raw materials are needed as well, like metals and plastics for zippers and buttons and dyes for color. And as with an electronic device, there are human resources required, like designers, advertisers, and seamstresses.

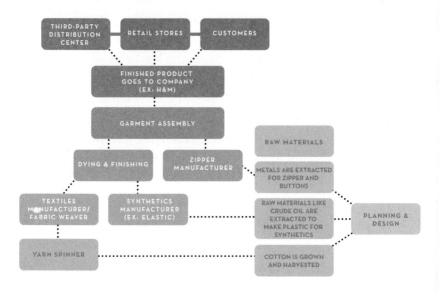

As you can see, supply chains for just one item can be pretty complicated. But at each and every step of the process, human hands are at work.

Behind Every Product Is a Story

As illustrated in the graphic, by the time a pair of jeans reaches your closet, it has been touched—literally and figuratively—by countless individuals. From the moment a cotton seed was planted, that pair of jeans and the materials used to make it have most likely traveled all around the globe, making either a positive or negative impact each step of the way. Even with our advanced technology and the role that computers and automation now play in today's manufacturing processes, there are still countless human components to every single thing we spend money on. Most brand-new goods have already lived an entire life before they even reach your hands. Behind every product is a story, and those stories have become very convoluted.

These stories are often hidden from us as well. Even though I don't personally know the farmer who grew the cotton to make the jeans I'm wearing, that doesn't mean that human connection is gone. I've just lost the awareness—or the consciousness—of that connection. Instead of being made down the street, our clothing is made overseas in a factory that we've never visited and can't even imagine. That factory is regulated by a government that may operate in a way that's completely unfamiliar to us, and with many of the manufacturing procedures managed by third-party companies whose names we'd never recognize. When you combine the complexity with the lack of transparency, we have virtually no clue about the story behind most of the products we buy.

Those working in the social enterprise sector must continue to ask ourselves how much we value the stories behind the goods and services we sell and the products we use to operate our businesses. We must strive to honor the work of everyone's hands. Looking closely at every level of our supply chains and acknowledging the humanity of those involved takes a lot of energy and a strong commitment, but it is foundational as we work to rehumanize people in our supply chains and honor the work of their hands. As we begin to focus on this core human element, we can quickly see how a small change can grow to have deeper impacts.

Social Procurement: Maximizing Your Social Impact

One of the best ways to maximize a social enterprise's impact is to buy from other social enterprises. La Terza's first passions were about purchasing coffees where we knew living wages were being paid to the plantation employees. So, when it came time to purchase branded shirts with our company logo, we knew we had to apply the same purchasing principles. Luckily, right after I began my work with La Terza, I attended a fund-raising gathering for a company called Freeset— now Joyya.com—and their CEO was visiting to share their story. As it also turned out, their US headquarters is based in Cincinnati.

Joyya is a textile company based in India, making shirts, hoodies, bags, aprons and other apparel items. They produce great quality products that are organically certified, but their social mission is employing women rescued from the red light district in Kolkata, India. By employing women who were forced into prostitution, they could give them new, meaningful, and worthwhile work, one person at a time.

Even though Joyya is a nonprofit organization, it was fascinating and inspiring to learn how they were able to use a typical for-profit business model as a foundation to lift up a specific group of people. It was also quite eye-opening to hear about the unexpected challenges that Joyya continued to face as they were beginning to have an impact. For example, at the beginning of their story, they would hire women and help them find new places to live so they didn't have to stay in the brothels. Inadvertently, what this would do is open a "new bed" for someone else to occupy. So, for every person they'd help rescue, a new person became enslaved. They eventually learned that it was better to empower people with meaningful work but allow them to stay in the bed that they knew to be their home. This also helped them to earn more trust with other women in this community.

I think this happens often with many social enterprises that are designed to support and uplift people in need. A for-profit business model of manufacturing was effectively used in helping people earn income in a life-giving way, but very quickly many new social support systems also had to be built or implemented in order to give a full foundation of one's basic needs. As one area of life was lifted, other areas of life were exposed that had equal importance to helping a person holistically.

Fortunately, I attended this meeting at the same time I was thinking about getting shirts made with our new La Terza logo. Using Joyya for the shirts we purchased was an easy decision. They embodied all our principles about sourcing coffee—from using high-quality materials to empowering makers—while also lifting people out of an unimaginable situation. They didn't even cost much more when compared to other top-quality shirts. But, beyond being aligned as businesses with a similar heartbeat and mission, our impact was casting a larger net. We empowered another group of people in another part of the world, simply by making a conscious choice of where to source our shirts.

A Powerful Ripple Effect

As you can see from our experience purchasing shirts from Joyya, when you purchase from other social enterprises, a very fast ripple effect begins. We were able to take a stand against modern-day slavery both in our coffee and our textile purchases. Our impact was magnified and the number of people we could empower increased. Once we realized the power that a ripple could have, we began to look for other areas where we could have an impact simply by putting more thought into who we were purchasing products from. Our company value of paying living wages to the workers of coffee plantations gave us a lens to look for other suppliers with similar goals.

Since we supply coffee to many shops and restaurants, we were beginning to be asked if we could also supply tea. Truthfully, we hadn't thought it was a necessary part of our business model and we were debating whether we should supply tea or simply focus our energy on providing coffee. But, the idea that we could again increase our social impact by supplying a new and requested product made the choice too easy.

Like coffee, tea is grown in many other developing countries, often with poor working conditions. Also similar to the coffee industry, there is an increased awareness in the tea industry to look at supply chains, build better relationships, and ensure living wages are paid to the producers. So, by finding a tea partner with our shared values, we could provide a product that was being asked for by our customers, create a new revenue stream for our business, and bring sales and revenue to another social enterprise, who could then empower other people in more countries around the world. And if I could find a tea supplier who was also thinking about how using their purchasing power could be directed toward other social enterprises, then the ripple effect would continue far beyond what I could directly see.

The impact of spending money for goods and services can far exceed a simple equal value exchange. The value of every dollar spent with a social enterprise makes an impact beyond an initial purchase. The more social enterprises there are to purchase from, the more all of our purchase can go toward social good. And the more that social enterprises buy from other social enterprises, the level of impact quickly amplifies.

Looking for other social enterprises to partner with also starts to become contagious. Once we found our tea partner, we began thinking about all of our purchases. From cleaning supplies, coffee-brewing equipment, service providers, and even office supplies, we began to look for vendors who were trying to make some kind of impact with their businesses.

In Cincinnati, we are fortunate to be near a vendor for office supplies that employs people who've become blind as adults, called Vie-Ability. People who are born with vision impairments can access immediate support and resources to navigate our world. For people who become blind later in life, this can be a tremendously devastating event. Imagine that you've lived a typical life, studied in school, earned a degree, entered the workforce, and love your work. One day you go to the doctor for an ordinary visit and you discover that you have a degenerative eye disease and that you will lose your vision in just a few short months. Your whole world crashes in an instant. You soon will be unable to independently drive wherever you want, whenever you want. You will not be able to use a computer or smartphone in the ways you know how to use them. You very likely won't be able to continue in your current career because for most of us, vision is a key component of how we have learned to do our work. For right or wrong, our work and our purpose are often tied together. It's one of the guiding values of this book! So, in losing your ability to work, you begin to feel a sense of purposelessness. Many other emotions come in waves, and you will likely face justified feelings of depression, anxiety, and fear.

These feelings were described to me by people working at Vie-Ability. But fortunately, their experiences turned into stories of hope. Vie-Ability uses the business model of supplying office supplies as a vehicle to teach people how to reengage in the workforce, learning new computer and light manufacturing skills. They happen to also be price-competitive, and offer next-day deliveries for nearly all of their inventory. This was an easy partnership to form, which again increased our social impact. We simply started an account online and products were delivered the next day.

TO CERTIFY OR NOT TO CERTIFY?

There is another tool you may consider to help not only clean up your supply chain(s), but also to show customers, clients, and competition that you've done so: get certified. Third-party certifications can provide a certain amount of weight; it's a way of saying "Our business is ethical in this way, and we've proven it to an objective third party against a fixed set of parameters." There are countless certifications out there, and each one has a different purpose and set of criteria.

Let's look at a few examples of certification organizations along with some of the characteristics of each, so that you can see how certifications might differ:

Buy Social USA: A great starting point that can help you verify your social impact, provide direction to become certified, and connect you with a network of other social enterprises to expand your social procurement opportunities with a low cost for certification.

Social Enterprise World Forum: Verification recognizes existing regional and national social enterprise verification systems; builds on existing knowledge and expertise; and provides accessible, affordable, and culturally responsive social enterprise verification in places where such options do not exist. The service aims to support the growth of the global social enterprise ecosystem and expand market access for all social enterprises globally.

BCorp: A certification that looks at the entire company's operations, as opposed to a specific ingredient or single product.

- Each company gets a "B Impact Score" to indicate how well it's doing and how much room for improvement remains.
- Renewals occur every three years.

Global Organic Textile Standard (GOTS): Ensures that the processing, manufacturing, and trading of textiles made from at least 70 percent organic fibers meet a minimum environmental standard when it comes to toxicity, wastewater usage, and more.

- A number of different third-party certifying bodies are able to award the GOTS certification (using the same set of criteria).
- GOTS mostly certifies textiles such as apparel and bedding.

USDA Organic: Indicates that ingredients and products are grown and harvested in the United States without the use of pesticides, fertilizers, hormones, and other synthetics.

- Certification can be awarded by a number of different third-party agents using the same criteria.
- Specific labeling rules must be followed whether the end product is "100% Organic," "Organic" (made with at least 95 percent organic ingredients), or "Made with Organic _____" (if at least 70 percent of the ingredients are organic).
- Certification needs to be renewed each year.

Fair Trade Federation: Many companies display a Fair Trade Federation badge as a certification, but it's actually a network.

- In order to be a member of the Fair Trade Federation, companies must meet strict standards involving living wages and safe working conditions, but membership is based on self-reporting and there is no third-party audit.
- Membership is renewed every year.

1% for the Planet: 1% for the Planet is also not a certification, but a network.

- Companies that are members of 1% for the Planet have committed to giving the equivalent of 1% of gross sales to approved environmental nonprofit organizations.
- Confirmation of donations is done annually.

GoodWell: This certification ensures that companies are treating their direct employees fairly and helps to measure the health of your company. One unique aspect is that GoodWell can help you gather data from your business, analyze the information, and identify actionable insights.

- Metrics include loyalty and engagement; pay equity (in areas such as gender, racial, and CEO-to-employee ratio); people and benefits (such as worker safety, benefits participation, and underage and part-time workers); and diversity, equity, and inclusion (such as hiring bias and organizational diversity).
- Renewal occurs annually.

Fairtrade International: Ensures fair standards such as living wages and safe working conditions.

- Third-party audits are performed by FLOCERT.
- Ingredients and/or final products may be Fairtrade Certified.
- A product does not necessarily have to include 100 percent Fairtrade ingredients in order to qualify for the Fairtrade label. Single-ingredient products may display a label indicating the product is fully traceable and meets the standards. A label with an arrow next to it, however, indicates that a minimum of 20 percent of the ingredients meet Fairtrade standards and that customers should check the packaging for more information.
- Differs from Fair Trade USA, a separate organization with different standards and processes.
- Renewals occur every three years.

A company may become certified for a variety of different reasons, and using certification as a means to clean up its supply chain can certainly be one of them. However, there are many considerations about becoming certified and it's important to take a look at some of the pros and cons when making your decision.

One potential benefit to certification is that it can be instrumental in building trust with customers and establishing your company as a leader in the social enterprise industry. It's a way of showing others that as an organization, you put your money where your mouth is, and are being held accountable for it. Additionally, certifications often come with access to a lot of helpful resources, which can further aid you and your company in making progress in all sorts of areas.

But there are potential drawbacks to getting certified as well. For one, you have to be able to fit it in the budget. There are costs associated with your initial certification, and then for each renewal, and those can add up quickly. It's not uncommon for small businesses, farms, and other suppliers to forgo the label even though they would meet the requirements, simply because they cannot afford it. Take our direct-trade coffee producer, Katia, for example. Katia operates a small coffee farm in Honduras, using organic and fair-trade practices. However, Katia's farm and community need a lot right now; primarily, the local school requires a significant amount of work and energy. Because of this, it's difficult to justify spending $1,200 of her profits on an organic certification instead of putting that money toward solar panels to power the school. La Terza cannot label Katia's coffee as "certified organic" when we sell it to our customers, even though it does technically meet organic standards.

Another potential drawback to certification is that sometimes it can be misleading. Companies are eager to show how they are making an impact for marketing purposes and some certifications indicate a step toward impact rather than full commitment. This may seem counter to what I previously said about how certifications can develop trust, but that's precisely the point: it's confusing. Each certification may have different requirements for a product to qualify for that specific label. And just because a product carries a certain certification does not mean it's perfect. If a product is made from a single origin and it has a Fair Trade Certified label, like coffee or cocoa, then it has to be 100 percent certified fair trade. However, if it is a product that has multiple ingredients—like a chocolate bar that includes cocoa, sugar, and dairy—then it has to have a minimum of 20 percent of the fair trade ingredient to earn the certification. This is a step in the right direction, and it should be recognized that the cocoa of a chocolate bar is in fact traded with ethical standards. But, it is important to note that the other ingredients used may not necessarily be sourced with the same standards.

Getting a certain certification may be a great milestone, but we shouldn't necessarily view it as the finish line. For example, certifying a cotton shirt as USDA organic is certainly a much better choice than sticking with the conventional route (which involves toxic herbicides, pesticides, etc.). However, we can actually go one step further: growing and harvesting cotton in a regenerative way.

Or let's use another example: organic milk. Certified organic milk comes from cows raised without antibiotics or hormones, who are fed an organic-grain diet. However, cows have not actually evolved to eat grain; they're supposed to eat grass. So, is organic milk better than conventional? You bet! Would grass-fed organic milk be better? Also yes. In this way, certifications may be better viewed as minimum benchmarks, as opposed to gold standards.

Everything we've discussed in this section cannot realistically be done overnight—it might take months, or even years. That's OK! If you find that your brand's supply chain needs a lot of work in order to be considered transparent and ethical, try not to be discouraged. The most important thing is that you take that next right step, even if it's just a baby one. Be honest with your team, employees, clients, and customers about where you are as a company, and where you're going . . . and then do what you say you're going to do. This kind of effort and integrity will take your business much further than you might think.

PLANT

Let's pause for a moment and reflect back on the woman sorting the beans that I met in Honduras. Her work in coffee is necessary for my morning ritual, but it's very easy to overlook how important her work is or even that it exists. It is a thankless and nameless job, but the job plays a role for so many of our morning routines.

One of the first things we can do to begin to incorporate this seed in our work is to pause and remember that there is a face behind everything we buy. A practice I have started and try to incorporate regularly is adding a moment of mindfulness when I'm at the store. These moments can be very small and take less than a second. They can also be a minute or two of reflection.

When I buy chicken breasts at the grocery store, I think about the employee who is standing during a long shift, cutting the meat that I'll be eating. And under my breath, I tell that person that I'm grateful. I also thank the farmer who raised the chicken, recognizing that being a farmer is difficult work. Finally, I thank the chicken. Its life supports mine.

The same practice can be used for many other things. When I buy milk, I can think of the dairy farmer who gets up at five a.m. to milk the cows. I also think of the cows and how their lives add to mine. Enjoying an amazing latte or a hand-dipped ice cream cone can give me the same moments of reflection. Nearly everything we buy, from food to clothing—shirts, hats, and shoes—are all made by people all around the world.

Think of our more complex purchases as well. Something like a car not only requires workers in the final assembly stages putting everything together, it also connects us to hundreds of supporting products. From tires, to radios, to the fuel we use, there are people hard at work bringing it all together so that we can turn a key and drive. I have friends who are engineers in the automotive industry, and they say that some of the production areas are as clean and sanitized as any hospital. Keeping production areas clean can help keep impurities out of the metals needed for car parts, which can help those parts be safer and last longer. Let's remember that behind this clean production area, people are maintaining its cleanliness, and they are playing a role in our safety.

The idea is not to feel guilt about the number of people behind the products. It's also not the space to feel bad about the circumstances that might bring people to different jobs that are unwanted or not glamorous. We are simply actively recognizing that there are thousands of people connected to the items we buy every day. Being mindful in this way can help us to have more gratitude toward others. It increases our understanding of how interconnected we all are to each other. And as we continue to practice mindfulness in our current purchases, it sets a new foundation for how we make our future purchases—both in our daily lives and in the items we source for our work. Adding a new practice of consciousness is a simple but foundational step in bringing in our new economy.

WATER

The next thing we can do is to begin looking for how we can have an impact with our everyday purchases. One can certainly begin by looking at a company's purchases, but I think it is easier to begin with our personal purchases, as they can help us take small steps in seeing how we can make a difference. Think of this as a new pair of glasses. When looking through the things that you buy, see them as not only something to consume, but also a way to empower others. When you do this, you suddenly begin to see opportunities everywhere. You might be surprised to learn that by making some small changes to our habits, we can use our purchasing power as a tool for impact—both as a consumer and in our businesses.

One of the reasons I was drawn to coffee is because it is a consumable product I enjoy almost every day. Not only can I have real and direct impact in helping other people around the world, I can also make a difference on a regular basis. Also, when I review the items that I buy regularly for me and my family, I see a lot of consumable items that can have an impact.

When I think about the videos of people helping animals that I mentioned earlier, it makes me realize that I want to make a difference. For me, a way that I try to embody this value is to look for free-range and organic chicken and eggs. I recognize that this is an animal giving its life to support mine, so I want to make sure that this animal also can live a good and healthy life. I want to know that rather than being raised in a factory farm, this chicken is fed well and has the opportunity to roam the way that nature intended.

Side note: I personally know many people who've become vegetarians for this exact reason—to support the lives of animals. I absolutely can understand and respect this idea. I also know that for me, eating a balanced diet that includes meat is something I need to do for my health and well-being. One of the best portrayals of how to honor an animal in providing food is the HBO biographical movie *Temple Grandin*. Her life story is inspirational, overcoming autism and radically transforming the cattle industry in the US. The reason she was drawn to make changes in the industry was to better honor the life of cattle, making sure that dignity and respect became a part of the slaughtering process.

Walking through your local farmers market is a great place to start thinking about changing some of your personal purchasing habits. Not only can you find local farmers who raise meat in humane ways, you can find other consumables that support your local economy and make a small difference, even within your family. Candles made with soy and natural fragrances are healthier for your home and can last longer. Soaps made with natural ingredients can be better for your skin and hair. Even granola and breads can be purchased that exclusively use whole ingredients that benefit our diets. These are all regular purchases that can have a small but significant impact.

I also want to note that this is a point of privilege and that often these items are more expensive than what you would find on your grocery shelf. I remember giving a roasterie tour to a local group of teachers a couple of years ago. They were first- and second-year teachers working toward their master's degrees during their summer break. I was talking about the positive impact someone could have by purchasing ethically sourced coffee. In that conversation, we talked about how one twelve-ounce bag of coffee costs $15 and that between my wife and me, we made one pot of coffee a day, which represented about a bag a week. As I talked about this, I could feel the mood in the room change. Rather than be inspired, the teachers began to feel like they couldn't make an impact, or at least make one without significant personal sacrifice. Changing their buying habits to include our coffee would need to be a budgeted item.

Thankfully in that moment, I could relate. Both my dad and my wife are teachers and I know that starting teachers often don't make very much money. I've never met a teacher who chose that profession for the financial reward—though I'd love to debate about why teachers should be paid more to match the value of what they bring to our society, that is a topic for a different day. The point is that nearly everyone I've met who became a teacher did so in part because of a sense of service and wanting to make a difference in the lives of children.

I was able to talk about three ideas that helped this group of teachers still think about changing their coffee purchases in a way that could have a positive impact. First, as we have talked about often in this book, I encouraged them to take just one step. If you're like these teachers and your budget is tight, maybe it's not about completely changing one's buying habits. Rather, it's about buying one bag of specialty coffee a month as a treat for the weekend or as part of a self-care routine, drinking an amazing cup of coffee when you also have a moment to pause and savor the experience. For this, you wouldn't have to make a significant change to your monthly budget.

Second, another way to approach this is to consume less and savor more. Globally, a single serving size of coffee is four ounces. In the United States, we increase that a little to be six ounces. Yet a small coffee at many restaurants is twelve ounces. Depending on what standard you use, this is between two to three servings of coffee. By drinking less coffee, we use less and therefore do not need to buy as much.

Finally, we talked about the desire to adjust our budgets. Sometimes, making a choice to spend more money in one area means spending less in another. I remember the first time I made the conscious choice to buy organic milk over conventional milk. For health reasons and hoping that cows would be treated more humanely, I wanted to make this change. At the time, conventional milk was around $3 per gallon and organic milk was $7 per gallon. Using about a gallon a week, my month food budget needed to increase about $16. This is not a lot of money, but at that time I was watching every penny spent pretty closely, so this did represent a night out at the movies. Like clockwork, the next week's grocery ad had conventional milk on sale for $.99 a gallon! It was difficult, but I had made a commitment and stuck with my new budget and purchasing decisions. Over time, as my personal budget allowed, I could introduce new items like organic chicken and eggs.

These same three principles can be applied to many other purchases as well. As I began to wrestle with these ideas and incorporate them into my personal purchases, I was wrestling with the need to buy new jeans. Learning about the inequities in the textile industry, I wanted to make a conscious purchase. Unfortunately, as I began to research various options, most ethically verified jeans cost between $200 and $400 per pair, which was a lot more than I was expecting to pay and more than my budget could handle. I also had an immediate need for a few new pairs of jeans. I made the choice to buy two pairs of jeans from a national brand with some shared environmental values. These were not the cheapest jeans available, but they were less than $100. They were also a brand known for a higher quality, so I hoped they would last a little longer. I also made the effort to start setting money aside in my clothing budget so that the following year, when I needed to purchase jeans again, I would be able to make a better purchase.

You can see in my personal example of buying jeans that I identified an item that I could use to make a change. I found a brand that could fit my budget, but I bought less than I was planning to, choosing to purchase two higher quality, eco-conscious pairs of jeans instead of four pairs of a lower quality brand. I "savored" these jeans in that I made sure to take better care of them and only wore old jeans for days when I was doing a lot of hard, physical work. And I set a goal to increase my personal clothing budget over time.

The reason this matters in our personal budgets is, first, that every dollar is a vote. More than ever, and with today's age of technology, businesses are paying attention to our purchasing habits. I remember a couple of years ago seeing a commercial on television about a breakfast cereal removing all GMOs and artificial colors from their products. The end of the commercial stated that "we want to feed you what we would feed ourselves." I honestly had to laugh when I heard that statement. It's not necessarily untrue that a company would change their products out of a new consciousness, but in my opinion, it would also be unlikely for a large company to change its behavior if customers weren't voting with their dollars. I think this company made the shift in their products because there are so many great options for buying healthier food. Within twenty miles of my house, there are over thirty farmers markets with access to healthy breakfast options. There are also many more natural, whole food options at nearly every grocery store. I appreciate this company's new direction, but to me it is clear that the habits of the consumer and all of our collective dollars spent inspired this change.

GROW

Incorporating new buying habits into our personal lives can help us build a foundation for how we look at purchases through our businesses and work. The new habits in our daily purchases also create a nice road map as we navigate new procurement policies. One of the reasons I enjoyed the farmers markets as an opportunity to change my personal habits is because they became just that—personal. I got to know people who were the farmers, bakers, and makers. I was able to hear about their passions, why they loved their work, what they hoped to accomplish, and the dedication to their craft. It also gave me the opportunity to ask direct questions. For example, I asked a fruit farmer if they used pesticides at their farm. They told me that for their apples they did, but minimized the amount as best as they could. They explained why apples were difficult to grow in Ohio without the use of pesticides, the detail about the pesticides they used, and ultimately why they made the decision to use them. At that moment, it was up to me, the consumer now better informed with new information, to choose to make a purchase that best fit my values. As business owners and managers, we have the same opportunity to match our purchases with vendors that fit the values of our organizations.

One of the best places to begin is defining how your business can make an impact. Maybe you have an opportunity similar to the one that exists with coffee and there's a natural fit, supporting vendors from around the world and ensuring people are paid living wages.

Once you identify causes your business naturally can connect with, a next step would be to make a list of all the vendors you use for supplies and services. We are a relatively small company, at this moment just hitting the one million dollar mark in annual sales. Every time we review our monthly expense reports, I'm in awe of the number of vendors we rely on to make our business work. From service support for coffee equipment, to general contractors like plumbers and electricians, to supply vendors for milk, syrups, bags, and boxes, the number of people we need to be successful is quite the group!

As you make this list, identify vendors that have an alignment to some of the values that matter. As in our story with Joyya, we knew were were fighting modern-day slavery in our approach to how we purchased coffee. Joyya was in a completely different industry but had the same ideals and values, so purchasing our shirts from them was a natural and easy fit.

The other lens to look through is to identify areas where vendors are available who are having a direct impact in a cause, regardless of exact alignment. Vie-Ability was a resource we could easily tap into that had very little to do with coffee or sourcing ethically. However, with a single phone call, we were able to utilize a vendor that had a direct impact with a marginalized people group. Essentially with no effort or additional cost, we expanded the reach of La Terza's social impact.

There are many other creative ways you can think about your impact. Staying local to different vendors gives you an opportunity to ask deeper questions, just like at the farmers' market. If you use services like web design, graphic design, or copy writing, can you ask about their social engagement and commitment? These are new conversations, so it could be that they've never been asked those questions. That also presents a great opportunity! You could tell them about your goals of using business to make social impacts and it could be a way they begin the journey themselves. There are amazing organizations like Girls Who Code or Innovation Girls that empower young women and minorities who historically have had limited access to educational resources in areas of computer science and website development. Maybe you can find a tech vendor who currently participates in a mentorship program or has a give-back model in its work. Or, as the vendor begins to learn how they can have a positive impact in their work, you could encourage how they could create their own social impact program.

Finally, one of the absolute best ways to think about your impact in your work is to network with other people. I have loved working with Social Enterprise Alliance. Through their network, I have been able to connect with others on their social impact journey and three clear things have happened. First, I have been able to make amazing connections with other social entrepreneurs, and through those connections I have realized that I am not alone. There are many other people just as passionate as I am about using their organizations to help with social causes. They have been a source of encouragement to keep going on hard days, and they have been there to celebrate successes with me as we have expanded our impact though our businesses' growth.

They have also been a great resource in finding other vendors and suppliers. Part of the network is that I've been connected with people I can purchase from, and who purchase from me. It's become a win-win situation, helping me to expand my impact and giving others a way to expand their impact through their coffee needs.

And last but not least, joining a social impact network has given me access to best practices. Our work is hard! Learning about what has worked and what hasn't from other businesses has been invaluable. It has helped me solve problems and find solutions much more quickly than if I tried on my own. I highly encourage you to check into your local or state social impact ecosystems to find like-minded people with the same heart. Conscious Capitalism, Social Enterprise Alliance, and American Sustainable Business Network are three organizations that have connecting networks and events throughout the United States. Good Market is also a fantastic global resource that can help you connect with vendors throughout the world. If you don't know where to begin, they are a great place to start.

As you get connected with these and other social impact groups, you quickly realize that you are not alone. There are many people beyond vendors who could support you. They are cheerleaders, confidants, commiserators, leaders, and teachers, all with common goals of making a difference in this world through business. Engaging with a network of like-minded people can be the single most powerful thing you can do as you think about your business and the impact it can make.

Seed 2

Employees and Team Members
Successful Brands Are Built by Happy Teams

Social enterprises cannot survive without healthy teams.

Our teams enable us to create our products and services, which allow us to exist and to serve others. So, just speaking practically, if a team can't work together well, either your business will suffer or you will not be able to have the impact you are hoping for. And why would you want to? If we're full-time, working forty hours a week, most of us will spend more time with the people we work with than we do with our closest friends and family. We should be prioritizing our efforts toward our team's health and enjoy being on our teams. Of course, we all have bad days, but overall we should look forward to going to work most days. And if we treat our team members the way we'd want to be treated, then we need to create space for them to love coming to work, too.

It's possible to exist and kind of chug along, and there will likely be seasons where your staff will find themselves overworked, or with a disruptive employee who is wreaking havoc on your culture. I've been there, too. But, when your team can thrive; when it's safe and can bring us joy, then our impact will also be deeper and be able to reach its greatest potential.

We're going to spend a lot of time in this segment giving you a number of tools to help you build a healthy work environment. Your team is your foundation.

———————————

Several years ago, a friend of mine had a baby; she had just finished her maternity leave and was heading back to work. She loved her job. She worked for a woman-owned company that was also a certified B Corp and had a strong social mission and vision. Not only that, she was passionate and extremely knowledgeable about the product and was really good at her job. She held a C-level position within the company, thrived in leading her team, and truly loved the people she worked with. Because her company was a start-up, she would often eagerly work sixty to seventy hours a week, helping put the company on a fast growth track while also progressing in her personal career. I knew that she cherished her time away as a new mother, but I also knew she was eager to reengage.

About a month after she was back at work, we met for drinks. I was excited to see pictures of her son and to hear how much she enjoyed being a new mom. Knowing how much she loved her job, I was also curious to ask how work was going.

"I don't know how much longer I can take it," she said as tears welled up in her eyes. "I'm completely burnt out. I've been overworked for a few years now—almost never taking breaks, days off, or vacation—and in some ways, I enjoyed that. I am very happy to be back to work, but I only had six weeks of paid maternity leave. That was a huge gift for a small company, but I really needed more time away. And then, when I did come back to work, nothing changed in regard to the demands of the work and my job roles. Yet, for me, everything has changed."

In an instant, I knew this would be a different conversation than I anticipated.

"I've never had trouble sleeping before in my life," she continued, "and being a new mom, of course I'm not sleeping as much. But right now, even when the baby goes to sleep and as I'm thoroughly exhausted, I'm lying awake in my bed and struggling with brutal insomnia, which is making everything ten times worse.

"I'm enjoying being with all of my coworkers again," she went on, "but we have a sort of 'always on call' culture. The more we work, the more we are respected and valued, especially from our owner. I'm trying to set new boundaries now—even just to unplug for the weekends—but when I show that I am unavailable, she just moves on to someone else in the company with elements of my job that I want to be a part of. So, on top of the normal stress, I'm also having a severe case of FOMO.

"The pressure is really beginning to build," she continued. "I am beginning to travel again, but with an infant at home, stress at work, and managing life on three to four hours of sleep a night, I am also wrestling with postpartum depression. I am doing all the right things—even paying to see a therapist and going to doctors. They have helped me to see that nothing will change if my stressors remain the same. I am really wondering if I should think about leaving my job."

I could sense that there was something more my friend was hesitating to say. "So, why don't you?" I asked.

"Well, it's just that the company is doing so many good things!" she said. "I really do believe in what we're doing, and in my work, I get to make an impact. Not only would I probably feel guilty leaving, but I also don't want to go work for some big corporation that isn't even trying to make the world a better place."

I deeply sympathized with my friend, and the irony of her situation was very clear to me. The company was clearly a social enterprise and held several trustworthy third-party cer-tifications, indicating its ethical operation. When it came to environmental responsibility and social welfare throughout its supply chain, the company was doing many things right. And even at a human level, there was a level of genuine care felt among the team. But, when it came to the structure of jobs, responsibilities, and an incentivized workaholism culture, it also seemed that there was a big component missing in pro-tecting the wellness of their team. Everything was always a high priority, goals were unrealistic, and motivators were not sustainable. There was an intention to care for the team and their mental health, but the job itself was set up to fail.

There was also something systematically wrong about a six-week paid maternity leave. From a small business owner's perspective, it's true that offering pay when someone is away for that length of time is a significant gift. It would be a finan-cial burden for many small businesses, as well as the hardship of a decrease in available labor. A small team would either have to absorb the work from a team member away, or a tempo-rary employee would need to be hired to cover the gap—which would be doubly financially taxing. Many women don't have access to paid maternity at all, so anything offered is a generous act. Yet at the same time . . . six weeks is simply not enough.

In this specific scenario, it was a woman-owned B Corp company that still lived within a patriarchal economic system and was limited in what it could provide for its female work-force. Many governments in Europe financially support maternity leave, while in the US the financial burden either has to be budgeted for by the woman and her family, her support network, or offered as a benefit from her employer. There is something inherently wrong with this system.

———————————————

Hearing this story and helping my friend process her strug-gles helped me to see that when a company begins the journey of becoming socially responsible, there are many other areas that also need to be addressed. I realized that a company could be amazing in some areas but horribly lacking in others. "Is this hypocrisy?" I began to wonder. How should we view a company that claims to be "responsible" or "ethical," but is then found to be negligent in one area or another? And what should be said about a business that is making such a positive impact globally, while its own employees are incentivized to overwork and suffer from the mental, physical, and relational consequences of a toxic work environment?

My friend's situation is difficult for me to reconcile. Even though I know I'm an imperfect boss myself, it's challenging for me to hear about a company that prides itself on certain values and ethics, while knowing how sick and undervalued its employees are. It leaves me once again with questions about how we define social enterprise. Does the mistreatment of its employees "undo" all of the good the company is doing in other areas? And if so, how much mistreatment would qualify as undoing? I don't think we should revoke this brand's social enterprise status because of this point of weakness. But we do have to address how much weight we should give the intentions of a company's leadership when the reality may not be fully implemented.

This situation raised many additional questions for me as well, like whether we should hold small businesses and corporations to the same standards, or do different sizes and structures of organizations get evaluated by different sets of criteria? My friend's company was in a start-up phase, which was both exciting and contributing to high levels of stress. It also meant that resources were limited, both financially and in the team's capacity. My friend continued to share that her owner was a wonderful person and they truly cared for each other. So, although there was an intention to have a healthy work environment, the reality of where the company was during that time was a barrier to implementing necessary changes.

Defining Good

Through my countless conversations about how we should define social enterprise, I've discovered that the impediment can mostly be narrowed down to one question: How do we qualify and measure good in the real world. Good is extremely subjective. In conversations with business owners, consumers, entrepreneurs, and managers, I've discovered that opinions on what qualifies as good—and therefore what kind of company could be considered a social enterprise—vary widely. Some hold a stricter definition of the term, arguing that for a business to be a social enterprise, it must put its social and environmental initiatives as the very top priority, even above profitability. Some even expect near perfection from brands in order to fit their bill of what a social enterprise is. Others take a much more liberal stance, stating that even if a company is contributing to a social or environmental solution in the smallest way, it could be considered a social enterprise. The latter definition casts a wider net than the former. I understand both of these viewpoints—as well as all the ones in between—and I believe there are benefits and limitations to each.

Using the example of my burnt-out friend, you can see how quickly the lines we might put around a good business can blur. Her company was doing amazing work, and yet had more work to do. Work boundaries needed to be set by both the employee and the organization. This would require deep conversations about expectations for each, and acknowledgment of the different stages of both the business and my friend's life. But, the reality is that many start-up businesses need a lot of attention and extra work. Different stages of life are similar, and certainly when a family has a child, there is a new focus that takes time and energy. So, how do we address the needs of both as we include thinking about a business's impact in relation to its growth? And more than that, how do we celebrate and acknowledge positive impact while also realizing that more work is needed?

Although it may be virtually impossible to find solid answers to these questions, it's an important conversation to have as we try to build a strong foundation for social enterprise. The one thing we can probably all agree on is that there is no perfect organization, and therefore we shouldn't expect to find one. If we are able to hold space for both the good and bad to exist next to each other, then perhaps we will have enough room to celebrate the positive while also having the courage to point out the negative and always work toward improvement.

I will admit that employee wellness wasn't really on my radar when I first came on board as La Terza's CEO. I was passionate and excited about fair wages and safe working conditions for coffee farmers, but I hadn't even thought about those same factors when it came to our own team. (Granted, the company only had two full-time employees at the time, excluding myself.) However, I soon realized that all the work I would do to advocate for an ethical and sustainable coffee industry would fall flat if I wasn't equally passionate about advocating for the people within La Terza. Not only would it make me a hypocrite, putting the validity of the La Terza brand and my own professional career at risk, but I also simply wanted to make sure that the individuals whose livelihoods I would most directly impact—not counting my wife and sons, of course—were happy and healthy. I wanted to make sure I didn't neglect employee well-being for the sake of the company's larger mission.

For a variety of reasons, today's workforce is prioritizing employee ethics more than ever before. Gone are the days when Americans were willing to clock in for forty years of their lives at a company that didn't care about them or saw them only as a number on an expense report. Most millennials and Gen Zers witnessed their parents' generation commit their lives to corporations in order to earn a paycheck, and they want something more. Additionally, because we have constant contact with our phones and access to email, it's easy to fall into a trap of always being "on." We are adjusting to how to unplug from our work in a way that was easier generations ago. It's not that companies necessarily care more for their employees than they did in the past, but these days, if companies want to attract and retain top talent, they must take employee well-being into honest consideration. If they are going to keep top talent on board for the long haul, managers must provide a culture in which employees enjoy their work and feel like they're making a difference.

Many businesses now offer different types of benefits such as remote work options, meditation rooms, and paid time off for employees to volunteer in their communities. It might go without saying that employers are now expected to take initiatives like diversity and inclusion, mental health, and pay equity very seriously. Today's employees want managers who care about their individual well-being, and they want to leave work feeling good about what they're doing. But it's not just for the sake of keeping workers happy that businesses should prioritize employee well-being.

We have just witnessed how important employee care is as we come out of the COVID-19 pandemic. In August 2021, at a time when companies were desperately looking for labor, 25 percent of employees quit their jobs and 65 percent of people were looking at other job opportunities.

There are many contributing factors to this migration: improving wages, managing childcare, seeking a new work schedule to match a family's needs . . . the list is endless. The reality is that because COVID forced many people to pause their work, when it was time to go back many people decided that the jobs they were working in were not worth their time and energy. This pause gave people moments of clarity to ask themselves what is genuinely most important to them, and they reprioritized their lives accordingly.

Perhaps no industry saw this more than the restaurant and service industry. Historically, this line of work has been known for long hours—often including evenings and weekends—lower pay, and high stress. At the time of this writing, it is an industry still trying to figure out how to attract and retain a new workforce. Many restaurants were forced to shorten their hours, or close on their slowest days of the week because they are short on staff.

The "great resignation" has sparked a shift in the middle-class workforce where many people have concluded they would rather go to a job without over investing their time, or overextending their mental and emotional energy into their jobs. Many people left their work and sometimes even their industries vowing never to return, looking for jobs offering consistent hours and pay, and giving more freedom and flexibility in their personal lives.

Happy Employees Are Good for Business

If you are an owner or manager of a business, one of the first questions that will arise regarding a focus on your team's wellness is the short- and long-term costs. And while it's true that many new programs will have an upfront cost, the long-term cost benefits can be significant. Employee engagement and satisfaction is crucial to the success of a business for many reasons, and the happiness of a company's team members is directly or indirectly correlated with:

Productivity levels. According to Gallup, in 2021, only 21 percent of the world's employees were engaged at work. Zoom out and we'll find that employees who are not engaged, or who are actively disengaged, cost the world $7.8 trillion in lost productivity. That amount is equal to 11 percent of the global GDP.

Customer satisfaction. It makes sense, doesn't it? Your employees and customers most likely have direct and regular contact with one another. For many companies, staff members are the face of the business and hold the power to directly impact a brand's reputation. If employees are happy, they are more likely to have positive interactions with customers, leading to customer satisfaction, repeat buyers, and word-of-mouth referrals.

Amount of turnover. Because of the resources needed to hire and train new recruits, it is incredibly costly when an employee leaves a company. Employee replacement costs vary greatly, depending on the industry and skills needed. Entry-level positions that require less experience and training will not have a high replacement cost, while highly skilled or management positions will cost significantly more.

Quantity and quality of innovation and creativity. An unhappy and disengaged employee will show up late, clock in, check a few things off a to-do list and then clock back out. Sustained creativity and prolonged innovation cannot be forced; rather, they spring from a well of meaning, purpose, and connection to one's work.

Costs of sick and stress pay. A January 2015 study from the CDC Foundation showed that "Worker illness and injury costs US employers $225.8 billion annually."

All of these factors ultimately add up to your bottom line. Kevin Kruse, founder of Leadx.org and author of Employee Engagement 2.0, tracked more than thirty studies that show how employee engagement correlates to decreased absenteeism, turnover, accidents, and defects, while also correlating to increased customer service, productivity, sales, and profits. To summarize his findings, he made this simple diagram:

Employee Satisfaction to Employee Engagement to Employee Ownership

The concept of employee satisfaction—also called job satisfaction—became commonplace in the 1930s when psychologists began regularly studying it. This was also around the time employers began regularly surveying employees. Essentially, employee satisfaction shows whether employees are content at their jobs, or like their workplace environment, compensation, and upward opportunities in an general sense. For a long time, measuring and ensuring employee satisfaction was enough. However, as our workplaces—and overall culture—have drastically changed, so has the relationship between employer and worker. Enter: employee engagement.

Employee engagement is a more modern term, appearing first in the 1990s and then becoming more widely used in the 2000s and into today. Where satisfaction has to do with employees' overall "happiness" in a job, engagement has to do with how committed and connected they are to their work.

Since the 2000s, employees had been in a transition as well, moving from a job that primarily satisfied their financial needs to work that was fulfilling in other ways. We entered a time where working for the weekend was no longer enough. People wanted to feel a deeper connection and meaning to work, work they truly loved. This was a contributing factor to how generations before us would stay in the same job for most their careers, to now people leaving their jobs and even career paths in order to pursue work with an added emotional connection.

Today, I think we are finding ourselves in another transition where employees are wanting to feel a deeper sense of ownership in the work that they do. They still need their jobs first and foremost to fulfill their financial needs. Secondly, they are seeking work that is emotionally satisfying. And now they are adding in the value of finding work that has a greater purpose. Many employees in this next generation are wanting their work to also make a difference in the world.

This isn't to say that these priorities weren't in us before today. For example, many public service professions like teaching, social work, policing, and firefighting attracted people who wanted their work to have an impact with others, often at the cost of less financial reward. Medical professionals and nonprofit organizations also drew people who wanted their work to have a greater meaning. The difference now is that this ethic is moving into nontraditional serving jobs. From bankers who are empowering marginalized people through micro loans to baristas knowing the coffee they are serving is helping to lift people out of extreme poverty, many more people are looking for purpose in their everyday work.

Ownership doesn't necessarily mean having a financial stake in the companies they work for—though I do think we will start to see a new wave of employee-owned businesses as a part of the social enterprise movement. This sense of purpose is connected to their sense of ownership in their careers. As I define ownership, it's about employees feeling like they are true stakeholders . . . that they are completely vested in the organization. Their work aligns with their needs and values, and now also includes work that supports their passions. In one sense, ownership is felt when employees have a direct say in helping create in their work. They want to be seen, have influence, and be valued. But ownership is also felt when they know their work matters. They want to be a part of something bigger than themselves and are choosing to work in places that offer these kinds of opportunities.

We are also seeing these same transitions in small businesses that are being started today. From creating jobs in order to provide for one's financial needs, to work that is enjoyed, to their products and services having a new depth of purpose, these owners are building businesses that offer the same fulfillment.

A couple of years ago, I met someone at a farmers market who had just started a small candle company. She excitedly told me about how her candles used essential oils and local soy so that people could have candles that were healthier for their homes. Many candles bought in stores today are made with ingredients that can add toxins and have a negative impact on indoor air quality. When she was finished telling me about her company, I immediately replied, "Oh, so you're a social enterprise!" She hadn't heard of the term before, but from my perspective it was clear that there was the greater purpose of helping people have healthier homes through each candle purchase. She just hadn't thought of herself that way because she was a for-profit small business and did not include something like giving back in her model. But it was clear that there was a greater meaning to why she started her business.

Needs to Values to Purpose

Our jobs and the needs that they have provided have been evolving through generations. A part of this evolution closely follows the hierarchy of needs proposed by the psychologist Abraham Maslow (see next page). At first, we need to make sure that our basic needs are being met. Jobs help us to put food and water on the table, provide shelter, and help our families with access to education and health care. This alone can provide the purpose and fulfillment needed for people to remain in their work. I have heard many stories about older generations who simply worked to ensure that their children and grandchildren could have better lives, and this was the fuel they needed to keep clocking in and out for their entire careers.

Throughout the 1970s and '80s, young people had more opportunities to pursue work that fulfilled more of our psychological needs. We were allowed to ask the question, "What would I love to do?" As the middle class grew, more people in our society didn't have to worry about having enough in order to survive. We were offered more higher educational opportunities and we were encouraged to pursue work that gave us a sense of belonging, prestige, or accomplishment. We were given permission to pursue work that fulfilled our emotional needs, and in part we still are given permission to seek it if we haven't found it yet. This is another reason we have observed a shift from previous generations in seeing more people continuing to change jobs throughout their careers.

We are witnessing this new version of finding purpose in our work, and it is a core value of many young adults who are preparing to enter or have just entered the workforce today. As their basic and psychological needs are being met, young adults are seeking work that enables us to find our fullest potential, which includes making a difference in our world. Workers may never reach the point where they feel they are making a significant difference, but it is most certainly becoming a part of their career pursuits. I will be curious to see if it may sometimes even leapfrog one's psychological needs. If basic needs are met, would finding work that has a deep purpose offer a kind of sustaining energy, even if we don't necessarily enjoy our work or feel accomplished?

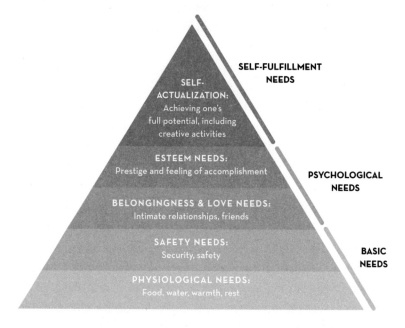

As business owners and managers, the question we must wrestle with is: How can we help our employees on the path of providing for their basic needs, incorporating their values in their work, and feeling a sense of ownership? For a moment, let's quickly think about all the employees throughout our supply chains, too. These are people we don't employ directly, but we do play a role in their employment. The work we hope to make available to them also aims to provide this same progression: to make sure their basic needs are met, to provide work that embodies their values, and finally to provide work that fulfills a greater sense of ownership and purpose.

A Holistic Approach

This seems silly to write, but our employees are people. The reason why that's so important to say is that people are incredibly complex. They come into work with their full beings. If they are stressed outside of work, then they will be stressed inside, too. If they are having relationship issues, they bring those emotions to work. If they are barely hanging on financially, they are bringing those worries to work, too. Gone are the days when an employer's job was simply to provide a paycheck in exchange for work. Looking at history through the lens of Maslow's Hierarchy, the employer used to be available only to provide our basic, physical needs. The evolution of work includes ideas of providing for our emotional needs—loving our work and aligning it with our values—to, dare I say, addressing some of our spiritual needs in creating work with purpose.

This might feel a little daunting to an employer. You might be thinking, "The resources needed to create good jobs is already a lot. Now we have to think about meeting emotional and spiritual needs?" Perhaps not. Maybe we have our own evolution too, in the growth of our individual organizations. First, we create jobs that provide for the basic, physical needs. But over time, we start to meet more of the emotional and spiritual needs. They can show up in the small moments of our daily work. Simply creating opportunities to actively listen and see our team members as people is a great first step. What I can say definitively is that it's worth pursuing how to meet these additional needs for the people who work with us.

Have you ever watched a sporting event where the momentum swings from one team to another? One team is leading and controlling a game, but then something happens. Maybe a spectacular defensive play from a player to stop the next score, or an improbable moment when a score—a home run, pass, or goal—brings a team back to life. The crowd begins to engage, and you can feel the energy shift from one team to the other. It's a special moment when that happens, and a team can overcome its deficit and take over a game—especially when it's the team you're rooting for.

What happens here? It's often not the physical side of the game that changes. The players from each team are the same as they were at the beginning. Both teams are athletic, highly skilled individuals who've played this game most of their lives. And while one team likely has different physical advantages over another, this does not always translate into a win.

Our emotions are a key ingredient in how our bodies perform. A team begins to "believe" that they can win—that they're going to win, and when that happens, the momentum shifts and all of a sudden everything falls into place.

When we believe in what we're doing and when our emotions are engaged with our work, the game changes. When employees believe in the mission, they tend to work harder. Their emotions are engaged with the mental, physical, and even spiritual elements of what they need to bring to their jobs and become the best version of themselves. Add the bonus of when an employee is seen and taken care of in terms of compensation, benefits, and the ability to have a true work-life balance, and the momentum of a business moves toward sustainability, growth, and impact.

Safety Is the Foundation

When we think about the steps in Maslow's Hierarchy, each has one key ingredient: safety. When we know that we are safe in each area, we have the psychological capacity to move to the next phase. When we don't have to worry about hunger, we have the ability to process our emotions and have better relationships. As we have better relationships, we can be in a better position to help others. So, as we reframe how we think about our team members and we expand how we provide good employment, I would suggest that we regularly ask how we can be creating safety in our working environments.

Striving to provide a living wage for all our employees is a great place to begin. Compensation is what allows the first building blocks to form, giving people what they need for food and shelter. One example of how to provide additional help in this area is by providing access to personal budgeting classes. When our team is stressed financially, it will affect their work and work relationships. Unfortunately, we all come from different means and have learned how to handle money differently. Some of us have a natural bent toward saving, while others are spenders. There are so many factors that shape our views of our personal finances, and some are more equipped than others to establish a healthy personal budget. All of that said, talking about money is also a very sensitive subject. Because it is so personal, we need to ensure that emotional safety is considered in this kind of idea. Offering access to a budgeting workshop could be a great idea, but it might be best to set it up outside of your organization. You can still play a role—maybe you offer scholarships to everyone on your team for classes in a larger area, but that are somehow anonymous. Employees would need the emotional safety of avoiding their employers' and coworkers' knowledge of their attendance, unless they wanted to freely give this information to others. This example shows the level of nuance needed to lean into what might be a good idea on paper, but also requires a number of practical and detailed considerations to be effective.

The #MeToo and TIME'S UP movements have also been incredibly important in exposing the true state of safety within many workplaces and the harassment that all too often exists within them. Anyone—no matter what gender, race, or sexual orientation—can be a victim of harassment or assault. Women and minorities are more likely to become victims, but it's important for companies to take action to make sure every individual feels protected. In part, this is an issue of ethics, but it also just makes sense that when someone doesn't have to worry about being a victim, they will be able to be their best selves and give their best to the organization. After all, your employees are there to work, so if they're experiencing harassment or trying to do their job in a toxic environment, it's not just that individual who is suffering. It's also other team members, productivity levels, and your business as a whole. Social enterprises are not immune to toxicity, so we should take the same precautions as any other company to ensure safety for all.

There are the obvious and extreme examples, such physical or sexual assault that can make a workplace feel unsafe. But creating safety can also involve more nuanced interactions. Here are a few attributes of a potentially harmful environment:

- Harsh communication; for example, speaking in anger or with a raised voice
- Inappropriate jokes
- Policies that are not followed consistently
- Office gossip
- Narcissistic leadership

- Negative cliques (i.e., "the boys' club")
- Inappropriate touching
- Disrespect of boundaries (physical or otherwise)
- Being too close and entering personal, physical space
- Unspoken implications or manipulation (i.e., guilt-tripping)
- Blatant harassment
- Inappropriate use of power

These are just a few examples of how easily a workspace can become toxic, and as a business leader or manager, you need to work to make sure these things aren't happening in your company. You may need to start by asking yourself, how do you even know if they are happening? The problem with many of these factors is that they may seem invisible and can easily go unseen by leadership. That's why it's important for managers to actively seek out answers and solutions.

The practice of active listening or creating space for listening sessions can help to improve understanding, inspire empathy, ignite compassion, and embrace the whole person. It is a practice in authenticity, trust, and a deeper connection. Make sure your team members know that if something is concerning them, they are free to discuss it with you or another appropriate team member. Don't be afraid to ask specific questions in order to grasp your company's culture from your employees' point of view. Be curious and try not to make assumptions or get defensive.

Of course, you need to be able to follow up the feedback you receive with actions. A friend of mine owns several veterinary clinics in the area, and recently his team of veterinarians approached him about closing on Sundays. They were feeling overworked, and even though there was a rotation to share the load, they had expressed that working this day too often pulled them away from family moments. A few meetings were held over a couple weeks to talk through the logistics of closing for this one day per week, including the loss of revenue. But rather uneventfully, my friend made the decision to close. When he told his team, they were surprised. They had assumed they would be heard, but that little would be done or even could be done to address their concerns. By acting on their concerns, my friend built a new level of trust with his team. Morale significantly increased among the staff and they felt a new safety in raising future concerns. A new awareness between both parties was created, and because my friend took action, he now has a trust to share feedback and concerns with his team, too. Additionally, the lost revenue was negligible and the cost was more than covered by the renewed commitment from team members enjoying their work.

The Value of a Well-Written Employee Handbook

Employee handbooks are generally viewed only as legal documents that lay the foundation of rules within an organization. A large part of their use can be providing safety among the team, in that everyone can know that the same rules and procedures will be applied to everyone. Of course, the key is that they are actually enforced. Workplaces may feel unsafe for employees if they are unsure whether certain policies will actually protect them. It is important to communicate these policies to your employees so that everyone is fully aware of their rights and of the consequences of being a perpetrator.

A thoroughly detailed employee handbook can also help to set the tone and cast a vision for your team. I have found that it is helpful to review these documents with your team regularly, usually on an annual basis, because it offers an opportunity to discuss the kind of culture we are striving to work toward together. We use this time to remind ourselves of the vision for the organization and our collective "why," as well as addressing policies that are working well and continually working on ways to improve. When done well, this exercise can lead to a better sense of morale, clarity, and focus, bringing everyone into alignment with shared expectations for one another.

I have even found it helpful to personify your employee handbook, thinking of it as a member of your team. Imagine that it's someone who embodies the personality of your business, and just like a person, it can be a living and breathing document that grows and matures over time. Like an employee, it needs time, care, and coaching. It can be a trusted resource both for you and your team members. I would even say that it could be a leader in your company, helping to guide and shape people and benefit everyone.

Using an employee handbook to help define a healthy team culture can help each of us on our paths of personal growth. We are humans, so in wherever we find ourselves interacting with one another, we unavoidably will find ourselves in conflict at some time. Most of us view conflict as a bad thing and we try to avoid it at all costs. But there is also significant value in learning how to have healthy conflict. In fact, learning how to have healthy conflict can lead to growth of many organizations. Disagreeing with each other well can lead to better business outcomes, improved relationships, and higher job satisfaction.

As employers, we can use conflict to learn from our employees, and we can also use tools like our handbook and management practices to be a guide in helping our team learn how to embrace healthy conflict. I've had this internal guiding challenge that we can use conflict to help our team members have better relationships outside of work, too. If we can reframe and learn how to have good disagreements with one another, pushing us to be better people, then maybe we can also inspire how to have better relationships with our closest friends and partners.

Finally, regularly reviewing company policies in an employee handbook can provide opportunities to make sure everyone on your team has the proper education. We are all learning and growing as a society, and we see this being captured in creating new policies and trainings for diversity, equity, and inclusion. We have so much to learn from one another, and embracing our many different perspectives is a great way to grow the safety we all can feel in our businesses—which in turn inspires creativity and a healthy culture. For these efforts, it's usually a good idea to hire outside professionals to conduct annual—or as needed—trainings in order to assure that all employees are very clear on what is and is not permissible in your workplace. Once again, this helps to create a sense of safety for our team members, and as employers and managers, we can create new levels of trust when we make conscious efforts to let our teams know they are indeed safe.

Diversity, Equity, and Inclusion

Americans and other global citizens are determined to root out systemic racism for good, and because our work is integral in so many aspects of our lives, it's important that workplaces also do their part to recognize and fight against systems of injustice. A common theme throughout this book is how the workplace has incredible power to drive change, so it's reasonable that we would also use our organizations and workplaces to address the implicit biases in our society, both on individual and collective levels. This, of course, is the right thing to do. It is also inherently good for business.

Throughout the height of the COVID pandemic, La Terza sponsored a podcast called The Third Place. My cohost, Mary Allard, and I would interview people and invite them into uncomfortable conversations. For a lot of people, learning how to expand one's world view can be awkward at first. In our immediate relationships, we are usually surrounded by people who look like us, so when we enter a space with others who are different from us, it can feel intimidating.

One of our favorite interviews was with Sara Blanchard and Misasha Suzuki Graham of the *Dear White Women* podcast. They believe that change has to be intentional and cannot come from complacency, and their podcast encourages becoming uncomfortable together as we learn how to talk about race. As part of their work, they provide an antiracism curriculum and have facilitated diversity, equity, and inclusion (DEI) workshops with many organizations. They note that DEI in business is an intentional decision that, when done thoughtfully, helps businesses grow and also makes every business a place where people want to work. A McKinsey study from 2020 shows that the more diverse a business's executive committee is, the higher the likelihood of outperformance. And sometimes, when businesses are new to the idea of broadening their (often unspoken) default idea of employees being white, heterosexual, cis-gendered, able-bodied individuals, they respond better to DEI initiatives when they understand that there is a solid business case for it. But to be truly successful, DEI can't just be about financials. As Sara and Misasha often comment, a business is not just an amorphous "being"—it's made up first and foremost of people who matter. That can be the employees, the third-party suppliers and distributors that a business is working with, or even its customers. The more viewpoints that are represented within the company, the more likely it is that it will be attracting everyone—both as employees and as customers.

A variety of points of view can only help an organization as it works to innovate and solve problems. As a middle-aged, straight, white man from the Midwest, my perspective on the world is limited. However, when I combine my perspective with the different perspectives of gender, race, sexual orientation, age, neurodiversity, and ethnic backgrounds found within members of the La Terza team, my perspective as a whole is so much wider and more valuable. My hope is that as our team grows, we will continue to expand our world view, which will help our business to grow, too.

How to Overcome Implicit Bias in the Workplace

We all have bias. This is the main thing I learned from another of my favorite guests on the Third Place podcast, Ryan Wynett. Ryan leads the Open Your Mind program at the National Underground Railroad Freedom Center in Cincinnati, and he explained that the word "bias" comes from a French term in sewing, and refers to cutting a piece of fabric from corner to corner, diagonally—at an angle or with a slant. It was a shortcut, finding the quickest path from one point to another. And as the meaning of the word evolved, the word was used to describe someone who was inclined to lean to one side. Having a bias is a natural thing, and because our brain is needed to process so much incoming information, it is hard-wired to make shortcuts often.

According to the Kirwan Institute for the Study of Race and Ethnicity at Ohio State University, "implicit bias" is defined as "the attitudes or stereotypes that affect our understanding, actions, and decisions in an unconscious manner." Appropriately, another term for implicit bias is unconscious bias, and the goal of learning about our unconscious biases is to bring them to our consciousness. Research has shown that these biases show up in organizations over and over again. One big misconception about implicit biases is that we should work to get rid of them completely. But again, everyone has implicit biases. They're a part of life and are completely unavoidable, so pretending that one is immune to them or denying their existence is a mistake, and it helps no one. Instead, we should first acknowledge that we may never be able to entirely shake our unconscious biases—although we can certainly decrease them—then bring more awareness to our individual and collective biases, and finally, take corrective steps to offset them.

The Kirwan Institute also identifies five key characteristics of implicit bias; the list is very helpful for our understanding:

- Implicit biases are pervasive. Everyone possesses them, even people with avowed commitments to impartiality such as judges.
- Implicit and explicit biases are related but distinct mental constructs. They are not mutually exclusive and may even reinforce each other.
- The implicit associations we hold do not necessarily align with our declared beliefs or even reflect stances we would explicitly endorse.
- We generally tend to hold implicit biases that favor our own in-group, though research has shown that we can still hold implicit biases against our in-group.
- Implicit biases are malleable. Our brains are incredibly complex, and the implicit associations that we have formed can be gradually unlearned through a variety of de-biasing techniques.

Here are some helpful steps to start overcoming implicit bias in your workplace:

Take a test. Harvard has developed an Implicit Association Test, which can be a very helpful starting place in opening your eyes to your own hidden biases. This test was

developed by professionals at Harvard with the goal of edu-
cating the test taker about his or her own implicit biases.

Practice mindfulness and self-awareness. One of the
most important parts of implicit bias training is to become
aware of it, and incorporating a mindfulness practice can
be a powerful tool for reframing our thinking. Becoming
consciously aware of your thoughts can help you learn
where your unconscious biases lie and regularly notice
when they come up. Only then will you be able to take
appropriate mitigating action.

Get feedback. A great way to begin gathering information about existing implicit bias on an organizational level
is simply to ask. An anonymous survey is a great place
to start. Using a Likert scale (a scale of one to five, from
"strongly agree" to "strongly disagree), a tool for analyzing surveys, prompts employees to answer statements such
as "I feel comfortable expressing my opinions in the workplace" and "I believe my performance is fairly evaluated."
Be sure to communicate that the survey is anonymous so
employees feel free to answer honestly.

Put systems in place. There are so many opportunities
throughout your organization—from the interview and
onboarding process to evaluations and promotions—to put
systems in place that can help account for implicit bias. Can
you require managers to interview a diverse group of candidates? Can you get rid of self-evaluations? Can you build
a diverse task force to hold everyone accountable? Can you
do blind interviews? Begin to build systems into your organization that can help evaluate, measure, prevent, and
correct unconscious bias—and then stick to them.

Use data. Good intentions don't always flesh out the way
we want them to. Leaders can have all the best intentions

and even be actively taking steps to ensure equality, but data has the power to tell the objective truth without unconscious bias underneath. That's why it's important to use objective data in our pursuit of an equitable future. Using a resource like that can be incredibly helpful in gathering and analyzing your company's data.

Evaluating Wage Gaps

Another incredibly important aspect of taking care of employees is addressing potential wage gaps. The three main gaps you'll want to look for are along the lines of gender, race, and position—CEO/executive team compared to median worker. There is an increasingly large number of companies releasing pay information—many are now required to by law—in order to improve transparency and accountability in this area.

Many still debate whether certain types of wage gaps exist at all, and I believe this is because the issue is much more complicated than usually acknowledged. We won't be going into depth in this book about all the nuances surrounding the issue; rather, we will discuss the high-level basics so that you are equipped to begin evaluating this issue for your business.

First, what do we mean when we say "pay gap"? The term is most often used in reference to gender. The gender equity gap refers to the lack of what we often think of as "equal pay for equal work." It is the amount women are paid in comparison to their male peers, statistically adjusted for factors such as job, seniority, and geography. The question to ask about the gender equity gap is: If a male and female with the same education and experience perform the same role in a similar location, are they being paid equally?

The median gender gap is the median pay of women working full time versus men working full time. This number more accurately measures whether women are holding positions of leadership. The often-cited statistic that women in the US earn eighty cents for every dollar men earn refers to the median gender gap.

Both of these numbers are important for different reasons. The gender equity gap is usually more straightforward, easier to measure with data, and a very practical starting place for companies and organizations that want to assess how they measure up in their gender pay equity. The median gender gap is more complicated and involves a whole host of influences, some of which we may not even know about or fully understand.

Many intangible questions surrounding culture and implicit bias factor into the equation, making the wage gap question nearly impossible to answer fully. This is where much of the controversy about whether the wage gap is real arises. For example, research shows that women tend to choose lower paying jobs, but why is that? It could be, as some research has indicated, that American culture steers girls away from certain areas of study starting in childhood, while we condition boys to perform well in areas like math and science—fields that typically result in higher paid positions. We also must evaluate the differences in wage gaps from country to country and culture to culture. A host of additional factors come into play as well. Some women may choose to leave or avoid higher-paying industries for fear of, or past experience with, sexual harassment, bias, and discrimination in the workplace. These are not simple questions.

Let's briefly look at a few other factors that could affect gender wage gaps:

Negotiation. Although women ask for raises as often as men, they don't get them as frequently. Perhaps this is a result of a cultural norm where women don't feel they can be as assertive with their boss for fear of coming off as "demanding" or "difficult."

Pay history. It's common for employers to ask about salary history during the interview process, but this practice has recently been found to perpetuate gender and racial wage gaps. In recent years, some states have even banned the question. When hiring a new employee, use metrics like market averages, job responsibilities, budget, and level of the applicant's experience to determine his or her salary. Leave the salary history out of the equation.

Lack of transparency among coworkers. There is a common misconception in workplaces that it is against the rules for employees to discuss pay with one another. Even though it's viewed by many as an offense that justifies firing, it's actually completely legal—and has been since the National Labor Relations Act was enacted back in 1935. Allowing workers to talk about pay makes many employers nervous, which is why so many of them still ban it. But if everything is aboveboard, employers shouldn't have too much to worry about.

Family. Of course, pregnancy and childbearing can significantly set women's careers back. Not only does a woman risk discrimination or even being fired for pregnancy, but also her compensation often suffers when she returns to work after having a baby. However, even childless women still earn less than men one year after graduating from college, proving that having a family is only part of the equation.

In addition to the gender gap, there are also wage gaps along racial lines. It is a result of the causes listed above, in addition to explanations involving how systemic racism has permeated our workplaces.

The Executive-to-Worker Gap

There is another pay gap we should be mindful of, especially as our businesses grow: the ratio between CEOs (along with other executive positions) and average workers. In 1965, CEOs made an average of twenty times more than their typical employee. In 1989, it was fifty-eight times more. By 2017, that average ratio was up to 312:1. For Fortune 500 companies, it was significantly greater, with the CEO of Mattel, for example, earning 4,987 times more than his average employee. That year, CEOs on average made $18.9 million, which was a 17.6 percent increase from the year before, while a typical worker's compensation rose a mere 0.3 percent. If the minimum wage had increased at the same rate as the average Wall Street bonus (not even including salary and other types of compensation), it would be over $33 an hour in 2019, instead of $7.25 an hour. To make matters worse, research shows that most of the time, the pay of executives isn't even tied to performance, meaning that CEOs are getting paid exorbitant amounts whether they're doing a good job or not.

While it's logical that a company's leadership should earn more than average employees, we can all see that there is a problem with the extremity of these differences. The economic gap between the bottom 95 percent and the top 5 percent of Americans has widened to an unprecedented level, leaving most of our GDP in the pockets of the wealthy few while the other 95 percent struggle. This rising inequality hurts everyone (even the rich): it can depress economic growth, lead to a rise in criminal behavior, increase health-care costs, contribute to severe political polarization, and more.

Most small businesses don't have to worry about this gap as much as large corporations do, but it's an important factor to keep in mind as you scale your business. If you purposefully set up your team's pay structure and strategy from the start, then you're much less likely to have to make corrections later.

Preventing and Fixing Wage Gaps in Your Company

Many of the measures we discussed above with regard to overcoming implicit bias can also be applied to preventing and fixing wage gaps. In addition to putting systems in place, asking for feedback, and using objective data, here are some more ways you can prevent and/or close any wage gaps in your business:

- Give immediate pay bumps where it's appropriate (i.e., if one employee is making less than another employee who has the same qualifications and is doing the same job).
- Intentionally recruit team members across racial and gender lines, especially for management and executive positions (where wage gaps tend to increase).
- Provide mentorship and training to younger employees so they have a clear path to executive leadership.
- Clearly define role expectations and career ladders with salary ranges for each rung.
- Ban the salary history question from job interviews.
- Foster a safe and inclusive work culture.
- Reward the lowest-paid workers with raises and bonuses before rewarding the executive team.
- Raise your company's internal minimum wage.
- Make pay scales more transparent for employees.
- Offer physical and mental health benefits fairly across the board.
- Be transparent about any gaps that exist and the plan of action your company is taking to close them.

Employee Ownership

Earlier we talked about the evolution of employees moving from a sense of satisfaction to engagement and then to ownership. We were describing the way a teammate would approach work, not necessarily about a financial investment. But one clear path that is tremendously beneficial for employees is creating opportunities leading toward an actual ownership stake in your company.

Basically, employee-owned companies are a way for employees to build into their retirement. They are invested with you, and in addition to their pay, they are able to earn dividends and equity in the organization. At first, this might seem like nearly all the benefits are for the employees alone, having little risk but participating in the reward. But, for a number of reasons, this is beneficial for everyone, including ownership stakeholders.

I have found that when you create a path toward ownership, you are also creating a newly energized, fully engaged workforce. A good friend of mine recently made the transition in the company he owned to becoming an employee-owned company, and he shared how surprised he was about the speed with which his business grew after the new structure was in place. He assumed that there would be a boost of passion in his team's culture, but he didn't realize how much it would positively impact the sales of the organization. Everyone enjoyed their work and talked about their jobs in their social circles, but once they became a part of the ownership, they all proactively shared with much more passion. "I gained twenty new salespeople without hiring anyone new," he exclaimed.

Employee ownership is a deeply empowering act. Social enterprises that set themselves up to be employee-owned often create a path to ownership for people who would never otherwise have the opportunity. Whether through a lack of financial resources, time, or know-how, workers would be hindered from starting their own businesses in a traditional setting. But this doesn't mean that these individuals should not be business owners, or would not have been owners had they had different opportunities.

One of the biggest reasons that I find success in entrepreneurship is because I had support systems throughout my life. I had family that supported me financially—both in helping with some start-up capital and in providing educational opportunities. I had many leadership opportunities in my childhood activities. Many of my needs in life had been met, which allowed me, following Maslow's Hierarchy, the space to dream and build a business. If you took any one of these or dozens of other factors out from my life's experience, many more hurdles would have been in my way to starting a business; some of them would have been completely prohibiting. I am grateful for the opportunities I have had but often wonder how many people would be great owners and business leaders had they been given same opportunities I had.

Carmen Dahlberg, founder and CEO of a marketing consultancy in Michigan called Belle Detroit, had built her social enterprise asking similar questions. She came to start this business after a successful career in marketing, leading creative teams from New York to the middle of the Huron National Forest. Her life and education provided the paths needed for this success and she wanted to extend that to others who did not have the same resources. Through Belle Detroit, Carmen is creating training programs, providing free childcare, and giving access to design software and laptops to young moms. She not only created good job opportunities for these women, she also provided access toward ownership and profit-sharing. The team is made up of women who love their jobs, get paid a living wage, and have a level of pride in their work knowing they are directly a part of an organization. Many of these women never dreamed they could be a part of owning something so special. Carmen's dream has allowed others to live a life filled with new possibilities, and she also has a team that is deeply committed to helping Belle Detroit grow.

Any organization can always work toward becoming employee-owned, but a very natural time to make a transition is when the owner is looking to retire or plan an exit strategy. A new season of life is upon the leadership of a company but they have a fully engaged and equipped workforce. Rather than selling to an outside buyer, the company can create a new legal structure to sell the business to its teams.

I am fortunate to live in a city with a nonprofit called Co-op Cincy whose mission is to help guide businesses in our region through this transition. Not only do they help create the operating structures needed for an employee-owned organization, but they also have funding available to help employees buy the companies they work for. They essentially become a bank between the employees and owners selling their companies, and help employees earn equity overtime though the dividends earned from the organization.

I recently participated in a cohort organized by Co-op Cincy that helped me shape La Terza's plan to become employee-owned. Through this group, I learned that a business can begin working toward the employee ownership model at any time, at any size. I am nowhere near ready to retire, and I even want to remain in ownership with La Terza for the foreseeable future. This doesn't mean we can't immediately start our transition now. We also don't have to hit a high dollar profitability point or have a minimum number of employees—both of which I thought were needed before I joined their cohort. Creating the structure of employee ownership can be done right at the beginning, too. There is no perfect moment. Even if it means setting growth targets and setting things in motion, you can start the process at any time.

Hiring and Firing

If you're in a position of managing teams, you've probably heard the phrase "hire slow and fire fast." The principle of this phrase is that we should take time getting to know new team members, allowing us the best opportunity to hire the right people. And then if a person is not a good fit—for the organization or for what they need to thrive—then it's better to part ways quickly before they become toxic to your team's culture.

The foundational truth of both practices is that they are about building trust. As you hire slowly, you are having multiple interactions and creating opportunities to develop trust between the new hire and you, as well as building the trust within your current team. I learned this the hard way. A few years ago, we were really happy with our team culture. It felt like the story of the Three Musketeers: one for all and all for one. We hired someone—not too fast, but also not slowly enough—and quickly realized they didn't quite have the same attitude toward their work as the rest of the team. They weren't directly detrimental to the business, but they also weren't really there for others in the way we expected. Relatively quickly, we set a meeting and through conversations with this person, each realized we had different goals and we parted ways. But there was damage to the trust with the current team. They needed to know that the next hire would be vetted with more time and intentionally. We needed to do a better job of protecting our culture and doing what we could through the hiring process to ensure they would be a great fit before they joined the team.

This also speaks to the trust of firing fast. Admittedly, I am still trying to work on how to fire more quickly. The example just mentioned involved about two months of meetings trying to change behaviors and attitudes before coming to the decision that parting ways was best for everyone, including the person who was let go. But, if I'm honest with myself, I knew before we began those meetings that he wasn't going to be a good fit no matter how many meetings we had.

I deeply value seeing the best in people and offering second, third, and even fourth chances. We all deserve them. The problem is, while this might be a worthy value on a relational level, it can have cancerous effects within a team. When they have to assume the burden for team members not holding their weight or coming to work with the same commitments, it is demoralizing. Even if subconscious, team members also start to care less about their work. If you fire slow and in the process lose trust from your team, the side effects can show up in lost production time, low morale, less productivity, and lost opportunity costs. Filling a day with numerous meetings to work through conflict is time that is not spent working. Not only is money spent in labor to work through these dynamics, there is also an opportunity cost of not growing the business.

Unfortunately, the principle of firing fast is not always an option. Firing fast means that you also have to spend time to set your organization up in a way that you can fire quickly. There have been times when I've had to fire slowly, simply because we couldn't afford the labor to stop. An employee may clearly not be a good fit, but often they are producing something. There is a reason they were hired in the first place and they can do the job they were hired to do in some capacity. For us, being primarily a production company, we needed to make sure that our customers were served and that roasted coffee was being delivered. Even if the labor wasn't the right culture fit, we needed to be sure there were no disruptions to supplying coffee. So, there have been times when we were not in a position to part ways with someone when we needed to. But what I learned is that we could still try to fire as quickly as we can. Once it is clear that someone doesn't align fully with your organization's values, quickly put things in motion to beginning the separation process.

Sometimes you have to hire more quickly than you'd like. If you find your business is growing too quickly, or if a critical team member puts in their notice unexpectedly, you may find yourself in a position where you need a body to fill the gap. If you find yourself in this position, one idea that you can use to guard against hiring too quickly is to hire with a probation period of three to six months. You can fill your labor needs but also give yourself an easy way out if the person is not a good fit. Likewise, this can give the employee an opportunity to learn about the company and see if the work is something they want to be a part of. Of course, this idea won't work in every scenario. If someone is moving into the area because of the work being offered, they will likely want an offer with more stability. And you still want to take some time to vet the new person. But this idea could be a good safety net for everyone.

Hiring slow also has a cost. When you hire slowly, that means financial and time resources are available to spend in the interview and onboarding processes. But these costs are short-term compared to the costs of hiring quickly. When someone is hired who isn't a good fit, the costs not only effect the team, but now you have to spend more time and energy starting the hiring process all over again.

Similarly, firing—whether fast or slow—has a cost, too. Firing fast is walking away from the sunk costs spent on hiring and onboarding and in lost production. But this protects others on the team, minimizing the risk of them looking for employment elsewhere outside of a dysfunctional team. In both scenarios, the long-term costs will always be less than the short-term expenses as you invest into your team.

One question that has guided me in the firing process is, "How do I fire well?" Many states are known as "at will" states, meaning that anyone can be fired at will for any reason as long as it's not related to race, gender, sexual orientation or religion. This does not mean you're not susceptible to liabilities or that you won't be responsible for unemployment benefits, but regardless, we should avoid using this avenue for firing at all costs. If someone is let go without cause, it will be a sign that no one is safe, and this will have a significant negative impact on your team. It is also the very opposite of how to "fire well."

I can remember the first time that I had to let someone go when it was clear they weren't a good fit, and even that we were holding them back. We had a series of meetings where we first talked through each of our expectations, how we were misaligned, what we hoped our expectation would be in moving forward. This helped us to see that we wanted two different things. Both we and the employee came the conclusion together. Then we went one step further. We talked about the things he had learned, asked questions about what he hoped a job could look like, and guided him in thinking about what he wanted his professional development to look like. While it was a difficult meeting, it was also a great conversation. We created an exit plan for his coming week and on his last day, he bought the team doughnuts and shared how grateful he was for his time at La Terza. This unexpected gesture confirmed that we in fact did "fire well" and was one of our leadership's proudest moments.

Transparency, Consistency, and Inclusivity

If hiring and firing are both trust-building activities, the focus of how to build trust requires transparency, consistency, and inclusivity. Throughout the employment life cycle, you want to strive for these elements as well, but they are accentuated in these beginning and ending moments.

In hiring, transparency looks like being explicit about what to expect from start to finish. This starts with how you write your job description and will include communication about the length and steps in your hiring process. Transparency will also include touchpoints for the interviewee and when to anticipate them, when you need to hire by, whom within your hiring or leadership team they may need to talk to, and what you will need from them in the different stages.

It's also important to let people know when they are no longer being considered for the position. This can sometimes feel awkward or difficult, but it is an act of being respectful to the applicants. It also is something you want to think about how to communicate well. I like to think of applicants as future customers regardless of whether they would get the position or not. Also, depending on how far they go through your interviewing process, they may be someone you want to consider for a future opening.

Consistency in the hiring process looks like having the same framing questions and processes for every candidate. Of course, follow-up questions will vary, but without the same starting points, candidates will inherently not be given equal opportunities.

Consistency is something to strive for with all your team members. It is an act of helping people feel safe. As a new parent, I have learned that being consistent is one of the greatest ways to show up for my kids. Spending time with them regularly, not allowing our emotions to exceed the moment, and creating boundaries like saying no and using discipline when needed all help our children feel a sense of safety, which is so important for their development. The same holds true for your team. Having a steady hand and empowering leaders to do the same will ensure safety, which leads to a team's development and creativity. It will allow them to be their best selves.

Once again, this speaks to the power of a well-written employee handbook. You and your leaders don't have to face unnecessary pressure to be a disciplinarian. The handbook contains the already agreed-upon rules for what behavior is good, what is inappropriate, and what corrective actions look like for each situation. Consistency means using the same corrective action plans for everyone, regardless of if they are leaders or key team members, or if they are in supporting roles like cleaning staff or administrative assistants. This also applies to the positive side, offering different tracks for professional development for everyone on the team. Consistency means no one is excluded or treated differently.

Finally, inclusivity in the hiring process looks like casting a wide net. Even if there is someone on your team who seems like a good fit for a different position, posting for the position internally and externally to a variety of places is a good practice. This helps keep your team strong too, because there may be some amazing candidates that apply with completely different and complimenting personality types, skill sets, and experiences. It could easily play out that a person internally is the best candidate for the next position, but by including a large reach externally, you could find a great candidate for the position your internal candidate is leaving open.

Inclusivity may also mean looking ahead and investing in hires you hope to make in the future. For example, in our part of the country, the coffee roasting industry is dominated by white men. Even when we cast a wide net, some of our coffee-specific jobs are bringing in only white male applicants. So, trying to draw from a diverse pool has proven to be difficult. For our head roaster, this has sometimes made him feel sad, isolated, and frustrated. He wants to work with others who look like him, too. So, we have tried to address this by partnering with local high schools with vocational tracks to teach coffee courses, entrepreneurship, and even how to roast coffee. While we can't address the issues of diversity today, we can ensure that when we are hiring five years from now, we have an empowered group of people to hire from.

TRUE EMPLOYEE WELLNESS

Making sure your employees are engaged and happy is not a one-and-done thing; it requires an ongoing process of evaluation and adjustment. It's best to put recurring systems in place, tweaking them as needed over time. Let's discuss some tips that will help you and your team do just that.

1) Start by reconsidering the status quo. These days, more and more companies offer perks like unlimited vacation, flexible working hours, and office goodies like Ping- Pong tables and unlimited coffee, snacks, and beer to boost employee morale and decrease stress. Although these perks can be great, I would encourage company leaders to be more intentional about the benefits they provide to employees. As we've recently discovered, some of these perks can backfire, leaving employees feeling obligated to never leave work. For example, some studies have shown that employees with access to unlimited vacation actually take less time off compared to those with more traditional vacation policies, and that unlimited time off can also lead to increased stress.

   I'm not suggesting that you definitely shouldn't offer these types of bonuses; they have great poten-tial when implemented purposefully. However, employers should know what's most important to their employees. If certain trendy perks come at the expense of salary raises or good health benefits, then those perks might be worth reconsidering. All the fancy amenities in the world can't make up for things like a trustworthy manager, opportunities for career advancement, and a safe workplace culture.

2) Ask . . . and then listen. How do you know what's most important to your employees? Assuming won't cut it; you have to ask. Don't be afraid to make yourself available, periodically sitting down with your employees and giving them some individual attention. Ask questions about how they're doing, how their work is going, and if they have any suggestions for improvement. Even if they bring up something you have zero control over, the fact that you took the time and energy to engage and listen can make a difference.

In addition to informal face time, it's generally good practice to request formal feedback annually, biannually, or quarterly. Put systems in place so employees feel they are welcome to approach their management with feedback whenever it's necessary—whether that's through town hall–style team meetings, regular one-on-one check-ins, or something as simple as a feedback box. Keep in mind that ensuring employee anonymity and/or confidentiality is always good practice in order to give employees confidence that they can give honest feedback without risk of repercussions.

How might you effectively and actively listen to your employees this week? If you're thinking about implementing a new program, ask what your team thinks before you spend money on something that could turn out to be a bust. If you want to show your employees how much you appreciate them, take a minute to inquire about what would make them feel recognized. Keep in mind things like differing personality types and working styles. What may work well for some people—open offices, for example—may be stressful and decrease productivity for others. Additionally, don't be afraid to ask your employees about their long-term goals, too—even if those goals are not related to work. Showing your team members you truly care about them as individual people and not just numbers or dollar signs can go a long way in fostering trust and increasing engagement. And remember, even receiving negative feedback can be a good thing if you think about the costs, stress, and turnover it will likely save you in the long run.

3) Serve the community together. Some companies let everyone take a few on-the-clock hours to volunteer as a team each month or quarter. A big part of positive employee engagement is making sure workers feel they have purpose in their work. Not only that, but they are more likely to feel good about working for a company that contributes to their broader community.

4) Recognize achievement. Everyone appreciates being recognized for what they do—even the humblest of employees. There doesn't have to be a ton of fanfare involved in telling your team members that they're doing a good job—although it's not a bad idea to put on an annual employee award show either. Through positive reinforcement and assurance they're on the right track, employees are more likely not only to enjoy their work more, but to go above and beyond the next time.

5) Mix things up. Adults like to have fun, too! Sometimes in our work, we can find ourselves in a daily routine that borders on monotony. One way to add excitement as a manager is to think through how you can bring some more life into your daily or weekly trainings and work processes. If you are presenting in a meeting, think through how you can present information in a more interactive way than slides and bullet points. Ask questions that encourage more curiosity, engagement, and collaboration during meetings.

6) Actively encourage innovation. Our employees are deeply integrated into our businesses and can be a tremendous resource for new ideas. Create space and encourage and reward employees for taking the initiative to share when they have an idea that could improve the company. Be sure to also thank them personally and give credit to them in future group settings.

7) Make sure you have the right managers. This is crucial. Research shows that half of workers quit their jobs because of their direct managers. That's a big number, and a lot of money and resources spent on turnover. A common mistake companies make is promoting the wrong people to management. Remember: Just because someone is successful in a certain role does not automatically mean they will be successful in managing that role. Most of the time, those positions require two completely different skill sets. To foster employee engagement, make sure your management consists of genuine, skilled leadership.

8) Provide coaching, training, and goal-oriented resources. Every employee has dreams of his or her own, both within and outside the company. Providing your staff members with coaching and extra training that will help them advance their careers or achieve their dreams can go a really long way. Take Jancoa, for example. This janitorial company had such high turnover that they decided to engage their employees by actively helping them achieve their dreams and goals, whether it was to purchase a home, get their GED, or quit smoking. The results: turnover plummeted and they found them-selves with a team of satisfied and engaged employees.

9) As always, be honest and transparent. Things don't always go the way you want them to. We all know that circumstances are sometimes outside of your control, even as the boss. When bad things happen, don't ever lie to your employees. If you need to, tell them you will get back to them with more information as soon as you can, but always be as transparent with them as is possible and appropriate. This is one of the foundational keys to trust, and trust is essential for employee engagement.

10) Utilize outside resources:

WELCOA (the Wellness Council of America) is one of the nation's most respected resources for building high-performing, healthy workplaces and is designed to help business and health professionals improve employee well-being and create healthier organizational cultures.

Lifeguides is an online resource that connects employees with Certified LifeGuides, matching with others who have similar life experiences in topics of personal growth, lifelong learning, and numerous life challenges.

Paid Volunteerism

As we begin to see employee wellness as addressing the needs of a whole person, we also start to see that work is only one aspect of who we are. Many aspects of our lives are found outside of our work. They are in our relationships, in our hobbies, and in many other passions. One additional way we can build into our team is to learn about other social causes they care about. And as you learn of other organizations that are important to your employees, you can also find ways to support those causes, too.

In my early carpet-cleaning days, I had one employee who worked with me for several years. He enjoyed his job, but let's be honest, cleaning carpets is unflattering and labor-intensive work. I had built the business to essentially "give back" some of its profits by empowering me to volunteer for causes. I wondered what it would be like to offer the same opportunity to my employee. He was volunteering at a local youth center for high school students and loved giving his time there. It was a great organization and I wanted to support it also.

One day, he asked to rearrange his work schedule so that he could take a day off and volunteer for an event. That was easy to do, but it gave me an idea for an experiment. He was an hourly employee, so taking a day off also meant that he wouldn't get paid, even though we moved the work into the following week. I was curious . . . what if I paid him for that day like I normally would, and we simply tried to add some of the jobs into the following week? If he didn't have to stress about an inconsistency in his paycheck, and he had time off to work for something he cared about, would he feel a sense of joy and happiness in his work because it allowed him to serve? And would that translate into being more efficient and focused in his time? To my pleasant surprise, this small experiment for this moment worked. Over the next two weeks, we were able to add in the jobs from the day off for volunteering and within the planned time of the originally scheduled forty-hour work week.

But this made me wonder about offering this regularly. He was appreciative of how we rearranged his day, and he seemed to be happier in his work, too. So, we tried it. He was volunteering about four hours a week for this organization, which meant he was giving an additional 10 percent of his time to a cause he cared about. I offered to match that time. This new experiment was designed to match his donation by paying for a full forty-hour work week, although he actually worked for approximately thirty-six hours.

Again, over time, this experiment worked. There were small fluctuations, but on average, we were able to complete the same amount of work in thirty-six hours that used to take forty. Giving my team member an opportunity to volunteer for something that was important to him seemed to help him be happier and more efficient. As a result, I had a very loyal employee and there was a new, unexpected way that the business could support the community.

I'm sure that this would not translate to a lot of businesses. His job was relatively simple, and some of the time made up was simply done by working a little faster in those thirty-six hours. You could even argue that I could have just paid more per hour or even based his pay on the jobs done in order to encourage a faster workflow. Either of these might have ended up with the same result, giving him time off to volunteer. But that said, I wonder if there is a truth to continue to explore here.

I was recently at a local B Corp networking event and one of the stories shared was that for four hours per month, one of the organizations paid their team to volunteer. Their point wasn't that work would be made up—they are a tech consulting company so four hours away means four hours not billed to their clients—but they were experimenting on how to have a ripple effect with their business. Their work inherently had social impact components, but they wanted to also be good citizens within their community.

In both ideas, team members felt heard and appreciated. Causes they cared about were also important to their employers. This helped them to feel a renewed sense of commitment to their work and to the companies they worked for. They also did truly have a direct impact in their communities. Multiple nonprofit organizations were served and benefited from this practice. The employees won by getting paid to do work they were personally passionate about. The employer won by having a more engaged and committed workforce. The community won because they were being served with much needed volunteer hours. Win-win-win! It doesn't get much better than that.

Lead by Example

Within the first year of owning La Terza, I was approached by someone with a process engineering background who was passionate about coffee and was looking for a career change. At the time, we were not in a position to hire anyone, but he said he was in a financial position where he could volunteer for a period of time to help us build out a segment of our business, which would help us earn additional revenue and ultimately create a job. I didn't want to take advantage of his time, but he insisted and together we mapped out how he could help us immediately while also creating the path for monetary compensation.

Over the next year, he and I worked closely together and would often brainstorm how to best position our company in the services we offered, our production processes, and our growth strategies. Relatively quickly, we created the paths for some compensation, but because we were a very small company compared to others, his pay was still well below his worth.

One day, he came into my office to let me know that he was considering taking a job in Seattle, the coffee capital of the US. It was going to be a great job, in the area of work he loved, going to a city he wanted to live in, and with a good salary. And while it would be hard for us to cover his workload, he had clearly found a great opportunity that was perfect for him. To my surprise, he told me he was wrestling with the decision and was curious about how I felt. To me there was no question about the decision to take the job, but he told me about how much he learned from me in my leadership and how we approached business. He did take the job, but we remain in regular contact and to this day, he often tells me that I was the best manager he has ever worked for and that he still applies all that he has learned in his current work and relationships.

The point is that while there was a level of sadness as he moved on to his new job opportunity, I know the time we spent together continues to have positive effects in his approach to work and leadership. This is often a conversation I have with coffee shop owners who tend to employ high school or college students for just a year or two. Rather than think of this as a negative and regularly having to train new staff, it can be equally viewed in a positive light. The season of employment is an opportunity to show what work could be. By modeling a team culture, strong and caring leadership, and transparent communication with your employees, you are setting an example that has the potential to stick with people for the rest of their lives. And when you do put in the work to building positive work experiences, the word will get out and you will attract new, high-quality employees drawn to working with you.

PLANT

We've all heard the phrase "If you want something done right, you've got to do it yourself." Unfortunately, I have learned this phrase to be an enemy of team culture. What I have learned about my personality type is that when I become stressed, I often default to stepping in and just dealing with whatever problem we are facing, usually shutting people out in the process. I also have to fight against my perfectionist tendencies. If businesses are made up of people—who aren't perfect—then businesses aren't going to be perfect either. Even if I could do everything by myself, I need to realize that there is strength and beauty in giving up control. And whatever project I am working on is only enhanced when I include others rather than turn people away.

Teams have to be bigger than you. You can't do it all. Sometimes, I wish you could. I have certainly tried. But in order to sustain and grow your impact, others have to be included. This also means things won't be perfect. They definitely won't be done exactly how you would do them. That's a good thing. There are always a number of ways to approach or solve a problem, and through empowering your teammates, you will have the opportunity to see things done differently and to learn new skills along the way.

Throughout this section, I've referred to the people we employ as "employees," "staff," and "team members." All are interchangeable, but I think there is a subtle but powerful shift when we begin to exclusively refer to our employees as "team members." They are partners with us. They help us on this journey of impact. They are integrated into many different aspects of our own work and passions. They may receive a paycheck from us, but they are more than their time clocked in and out. They truly are a part of our team—even in small ways they are a part of our lives, and they can begin to feel it when we use this language.

So, to plant is to change our view of the people we work with. They are a part of our lives. They share in our work and passions. They are on this human journey with us and in our work, and their paths intersect with ours. These moments we share with our team members are gifts that we can invest in, empower, and equip to expand on our work and passions. They also help us realize that we are not alone in our work. They join us in the collective effort of creating. And equally important, our team members get to just be human with us. I said at the beginning of this book that to be human is to work and create. An equally true sentiment is that the human experience is to "create with others." We get to share this life experience with the people we work with, and that is sacred.

WATER

HARNESSING PERSONALITY TESTS AS TOOLS FOR TEAM BUILDING

Personality tests have become one of the most helpful tools that our team at La Terza uses to foster healthy communication and relational dynamics between team members. You've probably heard about or taken a personality test at some point in your life, whether for work, for personal growth, or just for fun. For many years, the most well-known personality test was the Myers-Briggs, but the Enneagram has exploded in popularity over the past decade.

I've always been intrigued most by my Myers Briggs type, ENFJ. Specifically, I have been shocked whenever I test as an E or Extrovert because I absolutely crave alone time! I always feel like I need one day a week when I can have most of the day to myself to process my thoughts. Of course, there is a scale with each of these personality types—even the most extreme Extroverts need some alone time every once in a while. It wasn't until a psychologist friend pointed out how much I also process out loud with other people that I saw that I was truly an Extrovert.

The reason this was so important for me to know about myself directly related to how I lead my team. As an extrovert and someone who processes out loud, my conversations would shift throughout the day—as I was processing. I might start the day with sharing an idea with a team member to get their opinions and feedback. I would take their points into consideration and likely continue to form the idea based on what they suggested. I would then take the idea to the next team member and repeat the process until everyone had an opportunity to give insights and input. To me, this was great! Everyone got to contribute and the ideas would evolve into better ideas because of the team's opinions. What I came to learn from my friend is realizing the importance of saying to my team that I was processing out loud with them. You see, that first person who I first shared the idea with might not have realized that I was processing an idea. They often would leave a conversation thinking that an idea was solidly formed in my mind and we were heading in that direction. They had no idea that by the end of the day the idea could have changed and that the last team member I processed with heard a completely different initiative. The two team members heard two versions of an idea and I left them thinking two different things about where we might be going as an organization. Learning that I was in fact an extrovert who needed to process out loud helped me become aware of sharing that with the team, and helping them realize that we were not necessarily taking immediate action since I have just as many bad ideas as good ones. It also helped me realize that as an idea formed, I needed to follow back up with everyone to let them know where the idea was after talking with everyone involved.

PERSONALITY ASSESSMENT TOOLS

Here is a list some of the most common personality tests you may want to consider using to provide helpful insights and strategies for you and your team:

1) Myers-Briggs: Based on the ideas of psychoanalyst Carl Jung, this test sorts people into one of sixteen personality types according to four different areas: extraversion (E) versus introversion (I), sensing (S) versus intuition (N), thinking (T) versus feeling (F),

and judging (J) versus perceiving (P). If you've ever heard someone say something like, "I'm an INFP!", they were talking about their Myers-Briggs type.

2) Enneagram: The Enneagram sorts individuals into one of nine core personality types, from the "Reformer" (1) to the "Investigator" (5) to the "Peacemaker" (9). While people's Myers-Briggs profiles can change as they evolve, their Enneagram number is supposed to remain the same since it was formed during early childhood and represents their core fear. The Enneagram framework also provides insight into the "healthy" and "unhealthy" versions of one's type.

3) DiSC: The DiSC assessment is a personality tool based on the ideas of psychologists William Marston and Walter Clarke. It centers on four personality traits: Dominance (D), Influence (I), Steadiness (S), and Conscientious (C). Whereas the previous two tests are used in all kinds of ways, the DiSC assessment is primarily utilized in workplaces.

4) CliftonStrengths (formally known as StrengthsFinder): The CliftonStrengths assessment uncovers a person's unique rank order of thirty-four themes, such as Executing, Relationship Building, and Strategic Thinking.

Each of the above tests will generate a report that can provide invaluable insights about yourself and your team members that can then be applied to the workplace. For example, if I learn that my colleague is a I (introvert) on the Myers-Briggs, I will be much less likely to take it personally when she closes her office door for extended periods of time. If I learn that one of my team members is an Enneagram 9 (peacemaker), then I may consider utilizing his strengths for conflict resolution. Or, if I learn that I am highly dominant on the DiSC scale, then I know I need to be extra mindful of the way I give constructive feedback so that I don't come off as too critical.

Some of these tests even provide cross analyses, which can show you how one specific personality type will most likely communicate and work best with another type. These reports can be extremely helpful in so many ways, from shaping how we conduct team meetings and individual evaluations, to determining how we organize our workflow and set up our office space, to influencing the way we resolve conflict and set team goals.

Always keep in mind that there are no "good" or "bad," "right" or "wrong" personality types. No type is better or worse than another. Additionally, personality tests should never be taken as gospel or used to label people or put them into boxes. They are to be used as helpful tools, and that's it. These tests all have differing strengths and weaknesses, and some have been studied scientifically more than others. Take what is helpful for your team, and leave the rest.

One of my favorite assessment tools is a unique online platform called Cloverleaf. It combines the information from many personality tests, including variations of the tests from this list, and can help you see where everyone on your team is on each assessment. My favorite part of the platform is that you can receive daily emails with insights for both you and your team members about how they relate and process information.

GROW

A TEAM MEMBER'S TIME WORKING FOR US IS A GIFT

We have covered a lot of ground in talking about how we can grow and have an impact with our team members. This seed represents nearly 20 percent of the content of this book! There are several reasons for this, including the idea that we spend most of our time or energy with our team in helping our organizations achieve their impact. Our impacts and the ones we hope to continue to add simply would not be achievable without our own teams helping bring our products or services to our customers.

Creating a safe, happy, and thriving workplace culture starts at the top. So, whether you have one individual or thousands of people working below you, always act with integrity, and your workplace culture will follow. Keep yourself in check. Be humble if someone calls you out. Know what your values are and cling to them, even when it's hard. Give credit where it's due. Stand up and speak out when you see something unethical occur. Don't give out free passes to your favorite colleagues. Hold yourself accountable for making sure those in a minority are not drowned out. Take responsibility when things go wrong. Be transparent, genuine, and honest with your team as much as possible. These small actions, added up, can create great change.

Employee satisfaction cannot be an afterthought. When we prioritize employee happiness, everyone wins: not only your team members, but also your customers, your supply chain, your community, and the long-term sustainability of your business. I also want to point out that even if our organizations have direct and clearly defined social impacts, our greatest influence will always be found within our teams and the people we work with. Businesses large and small can be a model of social good by doing things differently in our approach to employee wellness. How we treat our team members, the culture we hope to foster, and learning how to best work through conflicts will have an ongoing impact that is difficult to quantify.

As we lead our teams through our own balances of integrity, strength, compassion, and our own imperfections, we are setting examples of how to live our lives to the fullest. In my opinion, the best leaders will always show characteristics of trustworthiness and authenticity, humility, continual learning and curiosity, and offering generous perspectives by assuming the best in others. The more we show up in this way, the more others will see how to incorporate these qualities in their everyday relationships. What you water, nurture, and put in the sun will grow, so even by just being our best selves and striving to grow, we will naturally attract others who are striving to be their best selves also.

Remember the friend you encountered at the beginning of this seed? She eventually worked with me at La Terza for two years and often reminded me how deeply and positively her perspectives about work have changed, with a large part due to working at a company that values her beyond what she can produce. By being a model of integrity and helping her to reframe her mindset of what work could be, she has established her own safe and healthy boundaries in her career, which has also helped her in other areas of life. She has learned and is continuing to learn how to balance her work, family, passions, and energy in part by being cared for through her job. And now she has launched her own social enterprise that empowers teenage girls. What a privilege for me to witness. Her time was a gift to me and our company and now her impact will expand beyond our work in ways I never could have imagined.

Seed 3

Customers
What Is Ethical Marketing?

Several years after I became CEO of La Terza, we went through a rebranding process. As a team, we sat around our conference room table and discussed the who, what, and why of La Terza: Who is our ideal customer, what does La Terza's company voice sound like, and why do we do what we do? These questions helped guide us in creating a new logo, as well as visual guidelines for our social media presence. They also helped us to answer what were the most important aspects of our brand, and how that comes through in our website, print materials, and interactions with customers. The question that stirred most debate was surprising: How do we communicate our social mission?

Ever since La Terza was founded, its social mission has been in the background of its public image. We didn't want people to buy our coffee because of our conscious mission; we wanted people to buy it because it's some of the best coffee they can find. It's not that we were keeping our sourcing practices and ethical standards under lock and key, but we weren't exactly advertising them either. As we met and talked though better communicating La Terza's values, half of our team members felt that putting more of an emphasis on our social mission was essential, while the other half felt strongly that to do so would actually go against the core of the La Terza brand.

Everyone did agree on one thing: we all wanted to highlight our commitment to finding the perfect roast profiles of some of the best coffees from around the world, and that truly phenomenal coffee can only come from farmers who are paid fairly for their product. But what would be our main selling point going forward: the quality or the social mission? While we can, of course, highlight both, deciding which facet was the higher priority was essential to nailing our overall brand. Is La Terza a socially conscious company whose coffee also tastes good? Or is La Terza a high-quality artisan roasterie that also happens to source its beans ethically? To an average customer, the differentiation between the two might not seem like that big a deal, but the distinction makes a huge difference in how the brand is perceived by current and future customers, employees, competitors, vendors, and the like. It is the rudder that steers conversations about our company, that dictates what goes into and what gets left out of our elevator pitches, and it ultimately plays a role in whether we gain a new customer. In short, it is the foundation on which our brand stands.

"To me, it feels a bit manipulative to focus on the social mission," one team member explained. "We're selling amazing coffee, not pity purchases and guilty consciences." It may seem a bit harsh, but he had an excellent point. Throughout my adult life, I've made more pity purchases than I can count, spending more money on a lower-quality product than I otherwise would have, simply because it was advertised as an item that did "good" in one way or another. In these cases, it was not the product itself that I was buying, but the mission. So, I could see what my team member meant about potentially manipulating our customers. It seems that there can be a very blurry line between sharing the story behind a product and using that story as the primary selling point to sway customers into buying something they may not truly want or need.

One of the most important aspects of operating as a social enterprise is its marketing and communication strategy. If a sustainable product and organization has a squeaky-clean supply chain, then it needs to be careful not to misguide its customers in its advertising in any way. It's crucial for social impact businesses to be honest with their current and potential customers about the ethics and sustainability of production, as well as the product itself—its usefulness, efficacy, and why customers would want or need it.

Recently, I came across a shoe company that advertised itself as "110% sustainable" on the home page of its website in big, bright, bold letters. "Oh wow, this company must seriously be going the extra mile!" I said to myself. But, when I looked around the website and product pages, I was sorely disappointed. Information about the materials and processes used, factory locations, certifications, and so on were missing. When I reached out over email to get some more information about the materials the shoes were made of, the answer I received said:

"We use recycled materials wherever possible—as of right now that constitutes about one third of the materials used. It's a starting point, and one we know will evolve. We are pushing our supplier as well as have a potential new material which will be 100% natural and will soon be on the market."

The brand representative went on to explain a little more about how the plastics they use are developed with minimal chemicals and therefore have a lower impact than traditional synthetics. "Although they are not perfect," he wrote, "they are a big improvement to the alternatives."

I certainly appreciated the clarity and honesty of his answer, but it also became clear that these shoes are definitely not "110% sustainable." I didn't buy the shoes. It's not that I never buy shoes that aren't made out of 100 percent natural or recycled materials—I do. Rather, it's that I felt the brand had been misleading on their website and they lost my trust. I'd rather give my hard-earned dollars to a company that says something like "Our products are 50 percent sustainable right now, and we are working every day to increase that percentage."

Ultimately, ethical marketing comes down to two things: honesty and transparency. In an age when consumers are constantly being bamboozled—told they need something they don't, or that something is better or different than it is—honesty and transparency is how you will set your business apart in the overall landscape, gaining and keeping customers for life.

When thinking about marketing strategies for social impact businesses, I often wonder if the best one is to begin with a clean slate. The message of traditional marketing and advertising seems to focus on how we are not happy people, but we would be if we bought what they were selling. Social enterprises don't need to create demand for something or communicate that "Your life will be perfect!" once you get this product. Social enterprises don't need to overpromise on anything. They don't need to hide information or promote half-truths. They don't need to publicly trash their competitors. And they don't need to manipulate customers in any way, shape, or form.

Instead, I think we should shift our focus and think of conscious marketing as simply sharing. As an exercise, think about what you would share about your company, its products, and/or services with your friends or family members. You'd most likely start by telling them about key features—the parts that are most important to you and/or the aspects that you think would matter most to them. You certainly wouldn't lie to them or lead them astray, as that would only jeopardize the trust you've built up in your relationship. You'd share the information in a truthful, informative, and maybe even entertaining way.

Similarly, social enterprises can use marketing and communications to enhance their relationships with current and future customers. You're simply sharing information about your brand with them in a clear and genuine way. Your ultimate goal is not just to get that customer to hand over their credit card today—it's to earn and cultivate long-term trust. If you do that, you'll create a win-win for everyone involved. Your customer will get what he or she actually wants or needs, and your business will not only get a sale, but also repeat business and word-of-mouth referrals. That means your employees and everyone involved in your supply chain wins, too.

One brand that does an outstanding job of this is Avocado Mattress. First, they start with a product that goes above and beyond in every way by creating a line of the safest, most organic, non-toxic mattresses that families can feel good about purchasing. Their prices are competitive and their customer service is excellent, with free shipping, one-year sleep trials, twenty-five-year warranties, and straightforward financing. By offering an exceptional product that's unlike anything else on the market, there is no need for Avocado to hold back any information, stretch the truth, or manipulate customers at all. They simply share the facts about their products. And they don't hold back either. There is a ton of information on Avocado's website, so potential customers can find out everything they need to know about the factors that are most important to them.

Once again, it comes back to the Golden Rule. Thinking about how you want to be treated when you are the customer is a great place to begin. Also, take note of how much transparency and agency you want from the brands you give your money to. As you answer these questions, they can quickly be a guide to how you communicate to your customers, both in advertising and in providing information.

Putting the Product First

One of the parts of my job that I enjoy but never thought I would is being a salesperson. I thought I hated selling! The idea of making cold calls or trying to convince someone to buy your product always made me cringe. However, I realized over time that I love to tell people about things that I love. To me, that was always very easy. It's like when you go to see a really good movie, you can't wait to tell others about it. The same goes for the things I purchase. When I find out about a great product, something new and innovative that I use often, or when something lasts a long time, it's very easy to let others know. Or when I have a great experience with a mechanic, plumber, or other service provider, I make sure to send people their way. I must tell a lot of people about these experiences more than I realize because I often find myself being a go-to resource for people looking for services.

Once I realized that because I loved my product and knew it was of the highest quality, I was no longer "selling" anything. I was simply telling a new friend about something I'd recommend to all of my other friends.

When I think about how I've wrestled with how to share the passions behind our social impact without overselling that story, I go back to our team conversation about La Terza's brand voice. We wanted to be known for amazing coffee. So, when I meet someone about buying our coffee, I begin there. Telling people about our social impact is simply a part of the story. It certainly is an important part, but it is not where I begin. Our solution to this conundrum is to create a truly outstanding product.

I realize that sometimes this is easier said than done. To have amazing coffee took years of classes and trial and error. Our team remains curious about learning new things about coffee and we constantly realize that we still have so much to learn! That being said, I do think a key to the Customer Seed is to focus on why you would want to buy your own product. I also believe that thinking about how you want to treat your customer is one of the most important things we'll discuss in this book. After all, customers are essential. Without customers, there is no business. And if there is no business, then you can't use it to have social impact. By starting with a product or service that is indeed outstanding and/or fills a gap in a certain industry, you'll be much less likely to run the risk of putting the story of social impact above the product itself, accidentally manipulating your potential customers.

This makes me think about Girl Scout Cookies. Why are they so popular—so much more so than, say, the popcorn you buy from the Boy Scouts or the chocolate bars you buy from local kids' sports team? It's because Girl Scout Cookies are delicious! Now, would most people buy cookies from adorable smiling children regardless of how they taste? Yes. In that case, we'd be buying the mission, not the product. Are we likely to buy more cookies because we genuinely love them and because Thin Mints are among the tastiest things in the world? Also yes. The Girl Scouts are not just selling leadership development for girls; they're also selling truly delectable cookies. They start with an outstanding product that customers actually want, and the story behind it just makes them that much better. Oh, and by the way, year after year between February and April, Girl Scout cookies sell more than Oreo, the number-one selling cookie in the United States.

As another example, let's look at the organic apparel company, PACT. Starting with just underwear, PACT began in 2011 to do what no one else in the industry was: making organic and fair trade affordable. Before then, consumers basically had two options: buy conventional underwear that involves potentially toxic chemicals at an accessible price point, or spend more, usually anywhere from two to seven times more, for organic ones. When PACT came onto the scene, they offered something that consumers wanted and could truly afford. The story of how the product was made was enough to sell the product, while the story of its social impact was secondary to the fact that it was simply a great product.

It's important to note that the idea of "quality" is only one way to have a strong value proposition. Customers also value things like convenience and cost. When my brother and his partner were planning their wedding reception, they thought through the table settings. Their wedding was in the summer, and they were having their reception in a newly remodeled barn. For their dinnerware, they tried to think about how to have a nice setting without breaking the budget. They were also hoping to keep things simple. They had found a great caterer for the meal, and having formal china and silverware didn't fit the atmosphere they were trying to create. They ended up finding disposable plates that were made from dried palm leaves. These plates were sturdy and suited the meal perfectly. They were also compostable, obviously being made from a natural product. Price and convenience were a higher value than quality. The product was also environmentally friendly which was its own version of having a social impact.

The Rise of the Conscious Consumer

The number of consumers who care about social responsibility has exploded in the last two decades. The term "conscious consumer" started showing up in academic literature in the early 1970s, continuing with a slow trickle through the turn of the century and then really gaining ground in the 2010s. According to a 1975 paper by the professor and marketing strategist Frederick E. Webster Jr., a conscious consumer is "a consumer who takes into account the public consequences of his or her private consumption or who attempts to use his or her purchasing power to bring about social change."

This definition still holds true. In essence, a conscious consumer is someone who "votes with their dollar" by assessing the social, environmental, and political impact of the products they buy. The number of conscious consumers is rising, with many people stating that sustainability is a major consideration when making purchasing decisions, and that they may even be likely to spend more on a sustainable product compared to a conventional one.

Here is where I backpedal—only slightly—on the argument I've already made about sharing your brand's social mission. As I mentioned earlier, we spent years putting La Terza's ethics and sustainability on the back burner when it came to marketing, choosing instead to emphasize the quality of the coffee. As time has gone by, however, we realize that we must focus more on our social mission. Why? Because that's what our customers want.

The term "consumer," it is worth noting, was rarely used until the 1920s, when it began a steady rise. Before that the word "citizen" was used instead. Around 1970, these two words exchanged places, with the word "consumer" used more often than "citizen" in the English-speaking world. What could these two words tell us about the way we view ourselves, each other, and our society? As psychologist Tim Kasser writes in the book *Hyper-Capitalism*, "Clearly, we now think of each other more as buyers of stuff than as participants in a shared society."

I believe the trend toward putting the word "conscious" in front of "consumer" is our effort to return to the idea of true citizenship. It's an acknowledgment of something we seem to have forgotten: that everything is connected. That we are still all participants in a shared society. That the choices we make about what we buy have direct and indirect impacts on other people, on the environment, on animals, and on entire ecosystems and economies.

Conscious consumers are the primary drivers behind the rise in ethics, sustainability, and transparency in business that we are seeing today. By voting with their dollars, using their voices in boycotts and marches, writing to their favorite brands, and exposing the often hidden truths behind where and how their goods are being made, conscious consumers are holding companies accountable and setting higher standards for everyone. For example, why does Walmart now carry so much more organic food than it did ten years ago? Because that's what consumers want.

Since an increasing number of consumers are explicitly looking for a social mission when making purchasing decisions, we don't want to leave that part of La Terza's story out. We are still careful not to prioritize the mission of our coffee over the quality, but we have found that if we don't communicate clearly about our ethics, we might be ignoring sales opportunities as customers may choose another brand that is louder about its positive impact.

Start with Why

In 2009, Simon Sinek wrote a book called *Start with Why*, explaining that the best businesses are clear about why they do what they do. The more clearly a business can articulate its "why," the more it helps attract loyal customers as well as great team members. As I read the book I quickly realized that for social enterprises, the "why" of their organization was very clear: There was a cause or mission, and through the purchase of the product or service, the consumer was able to play a contributing role. However, I think for social enterprises, it is also important to point out that your product or service needs to have its own strong and independent "why."

When I was in high school, I was a member of the marching band, and we were charged with helping raise money for new band uniforms. Like many school fundraisers, we had a catalog of products we were supposed to sell to family and friends. The more we sold, the more we could also earn points toward rewards and prizes. I always had a hard time selling these products, not because I didn't want to help raise money for the band—quite the opposite! I struggled because most of the items were average (or below average) products, and the price points were not that great either. These products were sold with the idea that whoever was buying them wanted to support the band. I would have preferred to simply ask people for donations rather than sell a poor-quality item that they probably didn't need. The candy bars we sold were NOT worth the prices we were selling them for.

I have sometimes noticed that social enterprises can fall into the trap of leaning too heavily into their social mission as the selling point for their products or services. Their "why" is clear, but the quality of the product or service does not match those of products in the market, or what they sell is significantly more expensive than a comparable product or service sold by a traditional for-profit business.

To be clear, I do not think that many socially minded businesses are trying to manipulate their customers by selling inferior products. I have found that almost to a fault, their focus is on their mission. That sometimes leads social impact businesses to forget the importance of having a great product or service that either supports or compliments their mission, but that also competes with similar products and services in the market.

One of the reasons I love Joyya (mentioned in the section on the first seed, Supply Chain) is that while their "why" is clear—to end human trafficking in India—their product also offers great quality at a good price point. Their shirts are organic and last a long time, and the materials are sourced with care and intentionality to be fairly traded and good for the environment. Their product "why" is strong enough to stand on its own. It's a great shirt! It also happens to support a great mission.

The Details Should Be in the Message

Within the first year of starting my carpet-cleaning business, I made the decision to primarily use green cleaning products. In nearly every home and business, I was able to provide a deep clean without adding any toxic chemicals to the environment. Only the most stubborn stains required conventional, more toxic products. This practice came at a cost. Not only were green cleaning products more expensive than conventional cleaning products, they required more labor and attention to detail. Thorough vacuuming, agitation after spraying the carpet with a cleaning solution, and proper rinsing techniques were necessary to give the customer the best cleaning experience. Basically, you can get great results by using organic cleaning solutions, but you can't skip any steps.

There were three motivating factors in using green products. First, I spent a lot of time outdoors and I wanted to play my small part in making sure not to cause harm to the environment. Second, I wanted to protect my customers. As adults, we can tolerate a certain amount of toxic load, more than young children can. So, I wanted to especially be sure that customers with small kids or family pets who were crawling and playing on the carpet soon after I left would feel completely safe knowing that their two-year-old could put their hand in their mouth without accidentally consuming anything toxic. And finally, I was personally using cleaning products on a daily basis. So, even though I was young and at times felt invincible, I knew that long-term exposure to even mildly toxic products was something I should avoid.

It honestly didn't dawn on me for a couple of years that I should tell my customers I was using green products. In my mind, it was just an obvious choice and not a selling point. It was the just the right thing to do. One day, I was cleaning someone's carpet that had a very stubborn stain; one that would require a more toxic, conventional spot cleaner. I felt an obligation to tell the customer that I could treat the stain, but that it would require something a little more toxic. I asked if that was OK, feeling that it was their choice to make and not mine. We talked through steps they could take to lessen the toxic load inside their home—opening windows to welcome in fresh air and letting the spot completely dry before letting kids or pets in the room. The customer deeply appreciated the information and chose to move forward with getting the spot cleaned. But then they told me they had no idea I was using green products and now they wanted to tell all their neighbors about us. It seems so obvious now when I say it out loud, but I didn't realize then that letting the customer know about my green commitments was really important.

As I started to incorporate our commitment to green cleaning products in my messaging to customers, I also came across a new term: "greenwashing." Greenwashing is claiming in companies' messaging that they are fully committed to clean practices, while not being completely transparent. These companies tend to commit to using green products in some areas for the marketing message while still using toxic practices in others. Even in my own messaging, I could not say that I was 100 percent green. I wanted to let the customer decide what cleaning products I would use in their homes. Many chose to move forward with having a small spot cleaned, but others would rather leave a small stain and not allow toxic products. Regardless of their choice and my commitment to environmentally friendly products in nearly all situations, I had to find a way to communicate that was fully transparent.

Complete Honesty Is Key

Greenwashing specifically speaks to misleading communication about environmental causes, which we will talk about later. But it is an example of the huge problem of deceptive communication about a company's social engagement. I believe that radical honesty should be one of the most crucial, nonnegotiable characteristics of a social enterprise, and unfortunately, as ethics and sustainability continue to gain traction in the mainstream market, I don't see this problem going away anytime soon. I'm worried that it will get worse before it gets better. In an effort to keep up with trends and the demands of consumers, some brands will continue to label certain products or the company as a whole as "eco-friendly" or "ethical" without providing much information about what that even entails.

When a company labels a product as "sustainable," what does that actually mean? One question very quickly leads to many others:

- What types of materials is the product made of, and what is it about those materials that makes them eco-friendly?
- Are they virgin or recycled?
- What sort of ingredients (like chemicals) and processes (like energy sources) are used to manufacture the products?
- What sort of packaging is used?

- What happens to the products at the end of their lives? Are they biodegradable? Can customers send them back to be recycled, repurposed, or refilled?
- What waste and energy-reduction policies does the company have?

These are all great questions that help us keep moving toward better sustainability! There is no one silver bullet but many ways to keep pushing toward being sustainable, and it will take them all to see sustainability fully realized. This is why one-, three-, five-, and ten-year plans for building upon the company's ethics and moving up the responsibility scale are so important. They set the long-term vision AND the steps and markers along the way.

When your brand makes an ethical claim, you want to make sure that it can be verified. This comes back to the idea that we want to treat our customer the way we want to be treated, which in this scenario means giving them helpful, factual information. Some customers will care deeply about digging in and doing the research. For others, you will have earned their trust, and they will expect that what you say is accurate. Regardless, we want to make sure that whatever message we present, it is pure and true. Especially today when misinformation is rampant, we want to empower our customers with knowledge.

Celebrating Right Where We Are

One common characteristic I find among leaders and managers of social enterprises is that we tend to be very values-driven, seeing the world in black and white, right and wrong. I think we inherently know that deepening our social impact is a journey and that we are constantly striving to be better versions of ourselves and our organizations. But because we are never perfect and often are looking ahead to see what other ways we could grow our impact, we don't stop to celebrate the milestones in the journey of our social impact.

I also think we're an optimistic bunch, having great hope that we can truly change the world through our business endeavors. We all love our products and services, but our greater passions are connected to the positive impacts we can share with others.

I believe both these characteristics to be important as they can be guides in how we lead our social enterprises and strive to become better organizations. Unfortunately, there are also a couple of drawbacks.

First, as we begin our work, passion, hope, and optimism fuel us. The work we are doing is hard! But, we know we are making an impact and are often willing to make sacrifices and go the extra mile. The problem is that when we aren't making impacts in the ways we thought we would, or as deeply as we had hoped, they can lessen our passion and drive. Ultimately, this can lead to burnout.

Second, because we are always keeping the social goals in mind, we can tend to present the future versions of ourselves and our organizations. We know the impact that we will have, and even if we're not fully there, we might be tempted to share more about what we are planning to do than share what we are actually doing at the moment.

I don't think these are necessarily bad things. We need to have a vision, and we absolutely should be sharing with our customers, teams, and everyone else our goals and what we are dreaming about in terms of impact. We just need to make sure that we are also accurate. We should let our customers know, "Here is what we are doing today, what we hope to accomplish tomorrow, and as we continue to grow, here are the areas of impact we hope to have."

Perfectly Imperfect

I think it's important to also lean into the idea that it's OK to be imperfect. Not only should we embrace this idea, I think it would be wise to celebrate it. One of the reasons behind the popularity of blogs and podcasts is that they are most often raw and authentic. The people who listen or read are drawn in partly because they relate to the content. None of us are perfect, so when we learn from others who sound like they are on the journey with us, there is an opportunity to feel more connected with the authors and their content.

Our social enterprises have the same opportunities when we embrace radical authenticity. By holding to our truths and not exaggerating facts, not only are we able to build trust with everyone we connect with, we are actually in a position of invitation. Our customers are actively seeking ways to participate in making the world a better place, and we all want to be a part of something special. By sharing our impacts right now while also casting an accurate vision of the future, we can grow our customer base by having them join at the beginning. It is true that this can be scary, especially when competitors may be having more impact that you might be able to at this time, but there is power in vulnerability. When you are vulnerable, you are also inviting and relatable. Again, no one is perfect (including that competitor who appears further along). So, let's invite all others who are imperfect to join in.

Having an understanding that we don't have to be perfect also encourages us to keep trying new things. Sometimes perfectionism is a barrier. If we know something won't be perfect, or if we have what we think would be a good idea without knowing how it would play out, we might find ourselves bogged down and not try anything new at all. Social enterprises need to embrace their creative spirit often. We are trying to solve big problems and for many, solutions don't even exist yet. Of course, we want to take calculated risks and minimize moments of failure as best as we can, but we cannot let the idea that things need to be perfect before we begin prevent us from trying out new initiatives.

The Brave, Authentic Journey

I understand, of course, why brands would be hesitant to share the less glamorous aspects of their operations, but I believe that radical transparency can be the way companies avoid greenwashing, build trust with customers and suppliers, and maintain integrity as a social enterprise. Being honest in how we use our words matters. Let's look at the difference between these two claims:

> *"This is a sustainable company."*
> *"Our team is working toward sustainability in every way we can, and here is how . . ."*

The first sentence indicates perfection, which we know is currently unattainable. It's also broad and vague, which can leave room for suspicion and distrust. This brand is now open to become a suspect of greenwashing. The second phrase indicates an overarching, long-term direction and purpose for the company. It's significantly more transparent and is much more likely to earn the trust of potential customers and other stakeholders.

I believe that a transparent journey is what sets true social enterprises apart, and it's why we will continue to return to the idea of transparency throughout this book. Radical transparency is both unique and brave. I would even say that this is a differentiator. We are all looking for ways to stand out in the marketplace, and a posture of transparency will help! It is rare to find a company that is open to sharing the good of what they do in addition to the areas that they want to improve on. Yet when it does happen . . . when we experience a brand that shares authentically where they are today and where they hope to go, a special trust can be earned with the customer.

To be clear, I am not proposing that we share the good with the bad. There is a reason we don't tell every person we meet our deepest thoughts. It would be a little weird and creepy if I shared how I was working to become a better person with the bank teller. This is true with our customers as well. They don't need to see our dirty laundry, nor do they want to know. We share those details with people who can help us work through them. What I am saying is that we need to be accurate and authentic about the good things we are actually doing.

Of course, there is a risk that being fully authentic can turn some customers away. Just like taking a risk in a friendship and sharing a feeling that is not reciprocated, a customer may prefer to look for another provider. However, in my personal business experience as well as stories I've heard from many other business owners, the number of customers attracted will far outweigh customers that might be lost.

PLANT

NOTICE BEING A CUSTOMER

As we begin to put the ideas of the customer seed into practice, one of the first ways we can embody these values is to be the customer. As you make your daily purchases and gravitate toward your favorite brands, ask yourself why you like them. The list of reasons why you might like a company can be endless. They can vary from simple to very complex.

I grew up very brand-loyal to the cars we drove, and to this day I am very loyal to several different car companies. In part, this is because of my familiarity with the mechanical design. Another reason is because I have now owned several cars that lasted well past two hundred thousand miles and a trust for quality with these brands has been established. But also, I have an emotional attachment to brands that I worked on with my dad. On reflection, I can see that my liking for a brand is motivated both by logical reasons and the emotional. I also notice that even though there are fact-based reasons for my loyalty, like when a car lasts a long time, the reality is that there are many brands that now often last equally as long and my emotional thinking is what seals the final decision. All of us have dozens of brands we like more than others. Paying attention to our own "why" behind the products we buy gets us to notice the role our emotions play in our purchasing decisions.

Specifically in our purchases from social enterprises, there is a deeper meaning behind why we are choosing a brand. They are often sharing their cause in their messaging, which calls on our emotions to be even more engaged. This is a good thing for sure, but when you are making these purchases, also notice the reasons you are buying the product outside of the cause. Asking how it meets your needs and matches to your quality and price point expectations can be a guide, too.

When they all align, you feel good and your loyalty grows. You buy a product that serves you and serves others. However, when they don't align—when a product does not meet your expectations even though you continue to value the cause you care about—notice how it makes you feel. You can certainly take an action: for example, you can let the company know that you care about them and the cause or causes they are working with, but the product did not meet your expectations. This can be very helpful to the company and could potentially open up a dialogue about how they can make adjustments and improve. If that were to happen, it would be a beautiful story and your loyalty to them would likely grow exponentially! But you do not have to take any action at all. You can simply notice how it makes you feel, which can then help you in designing your product or service for your social enterprise.

Noticing the emotions behind my personal purchases—both from conventional companies and from social enterprises—has been tremendously helpful in how I have built our brand, the services we offer, and how we share our company's values with our customers. We hold the messaging to our customers very carefully and with deep respect. We are earning the trust of the customer and that trust is sacred.

WATER

Earlier in this section we talked about the idea of "starting with why." And as we discussed, asking "why you do what you do" is a great exercise to begin to think about how to communicate with your customer base. In order to water this seed, I encourage you to take time to write down not only the primary "why" of your business, but also every other "why" that might come to mind for you personally.

I love La Terza's "Why": we empower independent coffee shop owners with best business practices because we believe that if more coffee shops and safe places to connect with others existed, we could positively impact the ways people in our society connect with one another. I genuinely dream of a day when the temperature of our political climate gets back to a healthy place. And I think that coffee shops that help people connect and talk through their differences can also help us all to see how much we have in common.

This idea is what drives nearly all our decisions. But, there are so many other "whys" that I enjoy. Many have already been discussed, like empowering coffee farmers in other parts of the world. I also love getting to meet so many great people—from customers to associates to industry connections. I love really good coffee and take a lot of pride in the efforts to perfect and hone our craft. This list would get quite long if I gave myself the space.

Writing everything out about why you do your work will help you stay true to yourself and to your customers. It will help be a reminder of what you are striving for as well. When you love your own product, it's very hard to not genuinely share what you love with everyone you meet. It keeps your value proposition high and when you do make mistakes, it creates space for you and your customers to give you grace in growing and striving to be better.

SWOT ANALYSIS

Another great exercise is to create a SWOT analysis, which is to list your Strengths, Weaknesses, Opportunities, and Threats. In our strengths, we write out the things we are good at and do really well. They could also be intangibles like having a great retail location, or a high profit margin. And of course, we do the same exercise with each of the other areas.

The point of the exercise is to get an honest assessment of what you're doing well and what you could be doing better. It can also be that sometimes, although you're better at something, an opportunity arises to put energy toward that rather than toward one of your weaknesses. We all have weaknesses and that's OK. A SWOT analysis will help you determine what you can focus on.

One interesting spin on this exercise is to also engage with your customers. As you make your list, think about what it would look like to get an outside perspective. It would most certainly uncover some valuable insights. You could start with asking some of your most loyal customers what they love about your company as well as feedback on things you may want to improve on. The caution would be that the customer is not always right, and they will not have as many details available to them as you have. So, you want to hold their feedback loosely. But knowing what a trusted customer thinks would be a gift for you and it would be a safe but powerful moment of vulnerability. It shows that you can be brave by asking for honest critique, which most often leads to even more loyalty.

MISTAKES HAPPEN

They will happen. And when they do, I have found that the best posture is to not shy away or hide from them, but rather to lean in and own them. People don't expect perfection, and mistakes are often an opportunity to connect and grow trust with your customer base. What can frustrate people or drive them away is when they feel they are being deceived. A sense of pride or arrogance often drives people away and can do significant harm to your company's reputation.

GROW

To start planting seeds in this area, spend a few minutes reflecting on these questions:

- How does your product or service compare to similar products or services on its own without the "why" of your social mission?
- Is there any way you could be overselling or greenwashing your product(s) or your brand as a whole?
- Are you making any claims (about ethics, sustainability, durability, effectiveness, etc.) without backing them up?
- Where can you afford to increase transparency with your customers? For example, could you add more information to your website?
- Can you clearly articulate the "why" behind your product?

Among those of us wanting to make the world a better place through our work, trustworthiness is a core value. I have noticed that being fully honest about where we are with our impact while also sharing where we want to go is a great way to build trust. It's OK that we are not where we want to be, and when we make mistakes, it's better to own them, learn from them, and work out ways to improve. Our company has been able to grow, not just in terms of sales, but in building better processes and systems when we have embraced healthy critique.

Seed 4

Community
Fostering Healthy Interdependence

One of my absolute favorite parts about running La Terza is the privilege of co-creating "third places" in and around my community. Originally coined by Ray Oldenburg in his 1989 book, *The Great Good Place*, the term "third place" refers to a community space such as a church, library, café, or park. It's not your home (your first place) and it's not your work (your second place). It's a third kind of place, a safe and neutral territory where all members of the community are welcomed, and conversation and play are encouraged.

The main reason I see third places as cornerstones to our society is because I believe healthy communities can lay a foundation for a healthy world. As our culture becomes increasingly divided, safe and neutral spaces are becoming all the more vital. We need places where we can come together to have complex, challenging, and sometimes uncomfortable conversations with one another . . . where we can connect with our neighbors and remember our shared humanity . . . where we can practice disagreeing with someone while also maintaining humility, curiosity, and giving others the benefit of the doubt. I believe that if we can consistently and effectively practice this in our local communities, not only could our national and global politics be transformed, but our mental health as individuals will be better supported as well.

Needless to say, coffee shops make great third places; people love to relax and connect over coffee. And although La Terza, along with our café partners, can play an invaluable role in our city by cultivating third places, not every member of our communities is a patron. Far from it, actually. Not everyone likes coffee or can afford specialty drinks. Some may prefer the taste of another company's coffee, while others need the convenience of a drive-through—which we don't have. Still others may choose to spend their time, energy, and money at other types of places for various reasons. However, just because those individuals are not direct customers does not mean they are not also touched by our business in one way or another. Outside of providing third places, there are so many other ways a business may affect a local community:

- Employing residents
- Buying materials and supplies from other local businesses
- Bringing in tax revenue
- Fund-raising for local organizations and causes
- Influencing community-wide regulations or political initiatives
- Sponsoring sports teams or other groups
- And many more

It's important for social impact professionals to acknowledge that businesses can and do impact their local communities in both direct and indirect ways. Those impacts can be positive, negative, or a mix of both. Take the coal companies in Appalachia, for example. For over a century now, large coal-mining corporations have settled themselves throughout states like Ohio, Pennsylvania, West Virginia, and Kentucky, profoundly shaping the social and economic landscapes for generations. On one hand, residents of these communities have at times been almost entirely dependent on coal companies for their livelihood, as these companies would employ entire segments of the towns around mines. On the other, the industry has wreaked havoc on the health of the residents and their natural environment. Mining is an extremely dangerous job. From 1900 to 1950, an estimated 95,000 miners died in America's coal mines from accidents related to explosions that trapped miners underground where they could not be rescued. Tens of thousands of other workers became permanently ill or disabled from mine accidents or black lung disease. With the increase in safety regulations and high-tech machinery beginning around the 1970s, the number of mining fatalities has steadily decreased, down to twelve deaths in 2019. The economic and environmental impact of the industry, however, continues to devastate Appalachia. Year after year, coal-producing counties land in the top 10 to 25 percent of the nation's poorest. It doesn't require much effort to link this economic desolation to the area's catastrophic opioid epidemic, which in 2018 claimed the lives of over seven thousand people in Ohio, Pennsylvania, West Virginia, and Kentucky combined. To boot, coal mining causes extreme instability to the environmental landscape, causing toxic, polluted water supplies, increased flooding, dangerous landslides, loss of biodiversity, and more. Higher numbers of several types of cancer; cardiovascular, liver, and kidney disease; and birth defects are also found in coal-mining communities. In 2011, the public costs of pollution in these towns were estimated to be about seventy-five billion dollars per year. Although the jobs provided by coal-mining companies have kept the lights on for many Appalachian families, it has been at great cost.

The coal industry, of course, is huge, and therefore, so are its impacts. La Terza Coffee could never hold so much weight in a community—positive or negative—in a hundred years. Yet, the way coal companies have shaped the communities in which they exist paints a picture for us and our smaller businesses. In the story of coal and Appalachia, we see how our existence can make a difference in a town—for better, for worse, or both. We see that the ramifications of our operations can snowball into larger issues that impact generations of people, some who may never even set foot in our stores, factories, and offices.

Creating Intentional Consequences

The way I see it, there are two primary ways a business can impact a community. Some impacts—like economic stimulation, employment of residents, and tax payments—occur almost automatically, simply as a result of running a business. By putting just a little bit of extra effort and intentionality into these processes, you and your team can potentially make an exponential difference in your community. For example, you most likely already purchase materials and supplies in order to operate your business. Instead of ordering those supplies from overseas, what if you purchased them from a local vendor instead? I mentioned earlier in the Supply Chain Seed that instead of using Amazon or Staples for our office and cleaning supplies, we use a company called VIE-Ability, a local business that employs blind and visually impaired workers. Especially considering that their prices are competitive with the big box and online stores, this was a no-brainer for us. We need these supplies regardless, and switching to a local company to make a small positive impact is well worth the minimal effort required.

The second way that businesses can positively impact communities is by going an "extra mile." This would involve taking an additional initiative—something that is not required to run your business. For example, your company might sponsor a fund-raiser for a local food pantry, or set up a working day with a local organization like Habitat for Humanity.

At La Terza, we work hard and take pride in roasting amazing coffee, but the question that drives us the most is, "How can we best support independent coffee shops?" We believe that coffee shops are critically important for the social health of our communities, and most people who come to us planning to open a coffee shop are doing it for the same reason. They usually love coffee, but more than that, the reason they are taking a risk and starting a business is because they want to create a space where people can gather.

I grew up being taught that you shouldn't talk to people about religion or politics, and have met many folks with the same upbringing. I now believe that to be a mistake. Politics and religion are easy topics to disagree on compared to our current hot button topics like how racism still prevails, figuring out how to bridge the financial gap between genders, finding real solutions for health care, and our border and immigration policies.

Given our current social divides in politics and our lack of ability to truly connect and have in-depth conversations on social media platforms, I believe coffee shops and creating a safe community space are needed now more than ever! For this reason, La Terza developed a coffee business course so that we could empower our customers to not only succeed in their businesses but to thrive and be pillars in their community for years to come. Even now, we are seeing our shop owners continue to take an active approach to creating community and teaching better dialogue by hosting panels of people from different backgrounds and perspectives. They are showing by example how to have deeper, respectful conversations.

I can vividly remember where I was when one of our shops first led a panel discussion. We supply a coffee shop in downtown Cincinnati called Black Coffee. It is a Black-owned business built around the idea that it should represent and celebrate the local African American culture. Their team had finished our course, had endless hours of training making great coffee drinks, and on their second day of being open, were hosting a panel discussion about what healthy gentrification could look like. The panelists represented different viewpoints and opinions, and this topic is one that has no clear answers. I was stuck in rush hour traffic when my Instagram feed notified me of this event. I immediately had to pull over as tears came to my eyes. "This is why," I thought. "This is why we do our best to support our shop owners like true partners." When we can give our best to our clients, they have more margin and resources to create the intentional space needed for their communities.

Our coffee business course was designed to help others create community. We have now had hundreds of participants and have been fortunate to help many shops open. As we continued to wrestle with how to build into our own community, we decided to pilot a program at a local high school, teaching students how to start a coffee shop within their school. Beyond teaching the numbers and logistics of selling coffee, the course teaches interpersonal skills and soft business skills. Taking personality assessments, learning how to form and manage a team, developing a brand and logo, finding a company voice, and using social media are all examples of different topics covered. So, while we are teaching about opening a coffee shop, we are also teaching entrepreneurship. Many of the students we taught in our first cohort were not planning to pursue a four-year college or university degree, but they walked away from this class having learned the basics of starting a business, and had a new experience that could help them build their own businesses later in life.

The possibilities of getting involved in your community are endless, and as you can see from our story, can also grow and evolve. Let your creativity shine. We started with the small question of "How can we best support our coffee shop owners?" We had no idea it would lead us to teaching entrepreneurship to high school students.

While some social enterprises may have more indirect or ancillary effects on their local communities, positive community impact is at the very core of other organizations' operation. Take the social enterprise Thistle Farms, for example. Based in Nashville, Tennessee, Thistle Farms employs women survivors of trafficking, prostitution, and addiction to make high-quality candles and products for skin care, home decor, and more. Not only that, but they provide supportive housing that provides not only a safe night's sleep but also medical care, trauma therapy, legal advocacy, community education, and family reunification resources. After two years in the program, candidates are eligible for graduation, and after the celebration, many women work full time for Thistle Farms while others take their skills into different parts of the community. Seventy-five percent of graduates are still living healthy and independent lives five years after their graduation. Although the brand offers exceptional products to their customers—I can attest to how luxurious their candles smell—the core motivation for Thistle Farms' founding was to fill a gap in the Nashville community. By giving survivors of abuse, trafficking, forced prostitution, and addiction a stable and long-term environment in which to heal, the Thistle Farms team is rising up against systems that commoditize, criminalize, and abuse women. In providing sustainable shelter, meaningful work skills, and healing space for individual women, the entire community has been and continues to be uplifted.

Take another organization based in Nashville: Trap Garden. Robert "Rob Veggies" Horton is an urban farmer and community health activist. He grew up in St. Louis, Missouri, and in his neighborhood there were very few fresh, healthy food options. Frustrated with living in various food deserts through-out his life, Robert started this social enterprise with the goal of providing healthy, affordable food to the surrounding com-munities. The Trap Garden team works with members of the community of all ages—from elementary school kids to college students to older community members—to educate and empower starting community gardens in order to provide for their own healthy lifestyles rather than depending on major grocery stores. This social enterprise helps to create jobs, pro-vides nutrition and education, and the very existence of Trap Garden is to serve the people in their neighborhoods.

Or take the Idaho-based B Corp indieDwell. In an effort to do something about the housing crisis that hit the nation after the 2008 recession, indieDwell began building modular homes that are sustainable—made from recycled shipping containers—energy efficient, durable, and affordable. The company has moved on to build emergency, workforce, and supportive housing, as well as college dorms—all to meet different types of needs in various communities around the country. These three enterprises are proving that running a successful business and serving one's community are not mutually exclusive.

The Interdependence of Businesses and Communities

Why should businesses go this extra mile, anyway? In the world of social enterprise, there is no place for savior complexes or pity handouts. We must resist any urge to ride in on our white horses to try and save our poor neighbors with our superior knowledge and preferable resources. Instead, let's acknowledge that every single member of our communities has something valuable to offer. It may be unconvetional wisdom that comes from a unique perspective or life experience. It may be a special skill or hard-working hands. It may be a new idea. Or it may be something else—something unexpected or outside the box, something that our capitalistic culture has not deemed "valuable." In this age of technology, we would do well to remind ourselves that humans are not machines. We are called human beings, not human doings. We must remember that members of our communities are not here to serve our purposes or to be cogs in our wheels. While I do believe that every individual has something worthy to bring to our communities and organizations, I also maintain that each human being has inherent value outside of whatever "merit" he or she may bring to the world.

A business owner's motivation to serve the community in which her business exists comes from an overarching understanding that, in the same way that "a chain is only as strong as its weakest link," a community is only as strong as its most vulnerable member. She understands that her business exists within a larger ecosystem; her business operations affect the community and the community's activities affect her business. They are not independent of one another; they are interdependent.

PLANT

I think one of the reasons the slogan "Make America Great Again" gained so much traction is that for many white, middle-class Americans, it was easy to visualize neighborhoods and communities portrayed in shows like *Leave It to Beaver* where the American dream was achieved when you had a house with a white picket fence, two cars, and two to three kids running freely in the yard. Unfortunately, this reality was not a shared experience for many Americans, including people of color and nearly every immigrant or indigenous people group. I always wondered if a more accurate slogan for many in this American experiment would have been "Make America

Great for the First Time," though that doesn't quite roll off the tongue or fit on a hat.

When I reflect on my 1980s childhood and what was different then, I remember life without internet, email, cell phones, and constantly being connected to everyone. Ironically, these points of human connection have also disconnected us. Yes, we are more connected than ever—and in many ways, that can be a good thing!—but we have also forgotten how to have more depth in our casual relationships. In suburbia today, we can drive home from work, open the garage door and go inside our house without setting foot outside and saying hello to anyone. It's possible, and maybe even common, to be neighbors without being neighborly.

It seems that many people are beginning to realize that the tech world we live in is missing a human connection element. Even as we talked about coffee shops being third places at the beginning of this section, most people who contact La Terza about wanting to open a coffee shop nearly always want to because they want to create space for their community. I do think the pendulum will swing back and that we're beginning to be good neighbors with one another again.

When we remember the foundational idea that businesses are made of people too, we can more easily see how businesses can also be good neighbors. Beyond the positive economic impacts that a business can bring to a community, they can also play vital roles in supporting our schools and children, raising awareness for causes, sponsoring local events, and setting examples of good stewardship. Immediately, the State Farm jingle enters my head, but I think it's appropriate to say, "like a good neighbor," your business is there, in the community and ready to help.

This relationship between businesses and community can also go in the other direction. There were many low points about the COVID-19 pandemic, but one of the highlights that

I remember is how many people realized that they played a significant role in making sure their favorite local restaurants and shops stayed open. During the first weeks of shutdowns, I saw communities purchase gift cards, change their purchasing habits by going out of their way to buy locally, leave significantly higher tips than normal, and show their support through social media about the businesses they wanted to stay open. There was a collective awareness that if you wanted to see the restaurant you care about be a part of the community after life normalized, then it was up to you as the consumer to play your part.

Of course, not all businesses survived, but I know that many did because of this new awareness. This newfound focus of local support reminded me of the phrase "It takes a village to raise a child." Similarly, we all learned that it takes a village to build a small business. Businesses and consumers are in relationship with one another. We need each other and we exist to support each other. As a business owner or manager, seeing your community as people you care about—regardless of if they are buying your product or service—can be a guide to help you think about the different ways you can show up with your community.

WATER

Paying attention to the small details can make an impact in how a business engages with its community. There are so many things that speak to people about who we are and what we value. From our actual products and services, to our branding colors, voice, and logo, even to the music we play in our retail spaces, we are communicating with our communities.

One of the common conversations I have with coffee shop owners is about their design and layout of their shop. We talk about seating arrangements and if there will be any small meeting spaces or kids' corners. We also talk about how the music played and our menu options can be opportunities to create a welcoming space. Being intentional with these details can go a long way to showing postures of inclusivity. For example, when you include gluten-, dairy-, and alcohol-free options on a menu, you are showing an awareness that you want to include people with intolerances to these ingredients.

Music, art, and food all can highlight specific cultures. Coffee is a great example of a product that highlights many cultures around the world. So, when offering a new blend from a new country, a shop owner may also offer food items from the same region. Music and art can present similar opportunities to celebrate different cultures. There is a beauty in our cultural differences, and the arts are a great way to highlight the rainbow of humanity.

There are many other ways to celebrate different cultures in our communities. Creating an inclusive space does not necessarily mean that you need to play a style of music with a broad appeal. No style of music will be enjoyed by everyone. It could mean that you have a genre that's most often played but rotate different kinds of music on different days or different hours.

It could also mean that you do only play one style of music to celebrate a specific culture but are still creating a welcoming space. I've mentioned that one of my favorite coffee shops in downtown Cincinnati is a Black-owned business that celebrates coffee, art, and music from the Black American experience. But the space is welcoming to all people. Whenever I visit, it is a full mix of cultures, many of whom are stepping in to support and learn something new about other people. It is truly a safe third place!

Our businesses all have a voice, and it can be used in so many positive ways to show solidarity. From our social media posts to the signs we hang in our windows, we can use this voice to support our neighbors. The voice of support can take on many forms. It can be playful—for example, when a sports team makes a deep run in the playoffs, a company's brand can change its logo's colors to match. It can also be very serious, a display of colors to support countries devastated by war or natural disasters. These are small examples, but just because they are small, don't discredit the power they can have. Businesses can play a significant role in our communities when they use their platform to amplify the voice of the voiceless.

So, the question becomes, who in your community has a voice that is not being heard? As you look into your community, seek out people in the margins, who have needs that are unseen or not being met. Providing support can range from bringing attention to those who need help to creating a welcoming space for people to providing paths of education, training, and employment.

GROW

As you begin to add an intentionality to how your business engages with the community, many more simple and practical opportunities will begin to present themselves. Here are a few ideas that can get you started:

Begin sourcing one or more of your materials from a local vendor: This also presents the opportunity to expand your social impact if your local vendor also has a social focus. Often, this can have a positive environmental impact by using less energy for transporting the goods you use.

Create a "Give-Back" initiative: This could be a temporary program, giving a percentage of proceeds to support various local fundraising efforts, as well as rotating and highlighting different organizations or causes each month. This also doesn't always have to be about financial support.

One of the best ways a business can give back is to take a day to volunteer for a local food bank, or an organization like Habitat for Humanity. Many organizations need helping hands as much as they do fundraising efforts. Of course, these can also be combined to maximize your impact and in helping bring awareness to the cause.

Talk to your customers and residents of the community: Listen, listen, listen. I am often reminded that we have two ears and one mouth for a reason, and that listening is one of the most effective ways to build relationships. It is the same for our businesses. Taking community surveys and finding a way for voices to be heard can make a huge difference in earning the trust of residents.

Engage with Youth: Connecting with teachers, classes, and after-school programs are great ways to get involved and show support to your community. You could be engaged with different learning and teaching opportunities, or also organizing volunteer efforts among young adults looking to support the causes that they care about. Other youth organizations often need support as well. Young adults can feel like their voice isn't heard or taken seriously. So, just as you want to create listening opportunities for the community at large, specifically listening to the next generation can bring in new perspectives and ideas. This may even tap into a passionate and underused resource to help bring social changes in your area.

Meet with local officials: City council members and government officials, educators and school board members, other business owners and nonprofit organizers are all deeply engaged in what the community needs. Much of the work is done behind the scenes and out of the public eye, so creating intentional connection points with these groups is a great way to learn more about how you could help.

Take initiative: Encourage ongoing conversations and invite others to join in solving specific problems in your area. Using your business as a physical space to bring people together to talk through different ideas can help generate a sense of unity around a problem, even if clear solutions do not yet exist.

Seed 5

Competitors
A Rising Tide Lifts All Boats

An Unexpected Insight

The day before my team and I left for the annual Specialty Coffee Association (SCA) Expo, I was working frantically to check items off my never-ending to-do list—as I'm always doing before leaving town, if I'm honest. Did I sign everything that will require my signature in the next week? Did I reschedule that meeting? Have all the systems been put in place so things can carry on smoothly without me? After a twelve-hour workday, I finally slumped onto the couch at home, exhausted. I sighed as the thought came to me: Is all this effort really making a difference?

It's not the first time I've asked this question. It doesn't come up often, but sometimes when exhaustion sets in, cynicism comes with it. I begin to wonder if maybe all my hard work is for nothing. After all, the news constantly reminds me of greed, power, and corruption; the ever-widening gap between rich and poor; the continual and terrifying decline of our ecosystems; and pretty much all that is wrong with the world. What difference does my measly small business make in the grand scheme of things? It can feel like I can't possibly make even a small dent in solving our world's problems. That particular night, I fell asleep with these frustrating questions rolling around in my head.

The next morning, my cynicism and I boarded the plane for Seattle, where the SCA Expo was being held that year. But, as I spent the next three days at the event, I was unexpectedly rejuvenated. My sense of meaning returned and my hope was restored by spending time with an unlikely group of people: my competitors.

I met and talked with specialty coffee roasters and shop owners from all over the country. Many of them were prioritizing ethical sourcing and the highest quality of production, just like we were doing at La Terza. I connected with roasters I knew from home—including from some of my biggest competitors—and we traded learning and inspiration that we planned to take back to Cincinnati.

As I reflected on my experience on the plane home, I realized that the discouragement I felt before the Expo had arisen at least in part out of a notion that I was alone in my work. I believed that my small team and I were the only ones trying to roll this boulder up the metaphorical hill that is social change. It's easy for me to get caught up in this story while I'm stuck in the day-to-day grind. I start believing that my team and I are on an island, and we're the only ones working to make a positive impact. Of course, I know this isn't true. But sometimes it sure does feel like it.

The realist in me says that perhaps it is true that I can't possibly put a dent in solving any world issues with my business. Maybe in the grand scheme of things my personal impact is so small that it's not even measurable. But, my experience at the SCA Expo reminded me of what I had forgotten: that I am not alone.

When I see the work other specialty coffee roasters are doing in their respective corners of the world, I'm reminded that I'm a part of something much bigger. Together, we actually might be able to compete with large coffee corporations, or even better: to pressure them to change their ways. I remember that when we join forces, we can move the entire industry—an industry that's worth over $225 billion in the United States alone—toward a more ethical future. A future where we can all thrive: from the coffee farmers and their land, to the coffee roasters and their employees, to their customers who want to enjoy a truly excellent cup of coffee each morning.

Competitors Are People, Too

Recently I met with a relatively new competitor in our area for coffee. He used to buy coffee from us for a shop he worked at, so we had an established working relationship. We talked about how things were going, the struggles we both had in gaining new customers as we worked through a competitive market, and about average pay in the area for different components of our work. It was a fruitful conversation and one I thoroughly enjoyed.

As he was leaving, he shook my hand and told me that of the other larger coffee roasters in the area, I was his favorite competitor. I was taken back by this comment, and it was one that I took as a significant compliment. It stuck with me for the following week, and as I reflected on why he said that, I think it was because I saw him as another human being and I genuinely cared for his success. Because much of our conversation was about wages in the area, I could see that each of our perspectives included the questions of how we could provide an income for our families as well as creating the same opportunities within each of our teams.

A Rising Tide Lifts All Boats

For the past decade, there has been quite a boom in the craft beer industry in Cincinnati. A couple of changes to our state laws helped begin the boom, which has now made Cincinnati one of the top beer cities in the country. At the time of this writing, there are more than eighty breweries in the city. They range in all shapes and sizes, from large distributors to nano breweries and gastropubs, finding their differences in styles and creativity.

Of course, there is also a delicate balance. It helps that Cincinnati has a strong German and beer-drinking history, which means there is an opportunity to serve many people in the community. I also know that not every brewery plays nice, and I'm sure there have been some enemies made along the way. But it is clear that a part of the success of this community is that they build into each other, even if unintentionally. Our city has begun to gain national attention, inviting visitors and others in the industry to take notice. And even with a high number of breweries in a small city, there are surprisingly still opportunities for more.

We see the idea of a rising tide play out often once we begin to take notice. For example, it's very common for competing car dealerships to be located together in an area of town. While there can be times when you see single businesses in an area, more often there will be a cluster, even though they are in competition. This attracts car buyers to a single area because it makes it easier to compare different makes and models. The same is true with restaurants. Several communities in my area have experienced a resurgence in their city centers. It's not because one restaurant has recently opened to grab headlines; rather, there are several to choose from that have attracted many new faces to the community.

Some areas of the country become known for a common product or experience. They are in competition with one another, but collectively, they make these areas special. Napa Valley, California, is known for its amazing wineries. Aspen, Colorado, is known for its incredible skiing. These clusters of competitors have defined the landscape of their communities, building each other up in the process.

Zooming Out to View Loftier Goals

I will admit it: This seed makes me quite uncomfortable at times. Although competition is a crucial part of what makes a free market work, I'm not exactly excited to welcome my own competitors with open arms. It's easy to understand why: When someone rolls up on the scene with the same idea—or maybe even a better one—it's a threat. You start thinking: Will they take some of our customers, or threaten the success of our business?

This makes it easy to see our competition as "the enemy," and our culture often highlights the negativity of being highly competitive. We see this play out often in sports rivalries that can cross the line from healthy competition to an ugliness when respect for an opponent is lost and a genuine animosity is displayed. Thankfully, they can also show us what good sportsmanship looks like. There is a reason moments captured on video when an injured athlete is helped across a finish line by a healthy competitor become the most downloaded and inspiring moments shared online. These moments humanize our pains and our greatest achievements. Sports embody the competitive spirit within us, while most often also sharing and humanizing the pain of defeat.

Sports is just one example of how our culture teaches us that we have to gain the upper hand over our competition. Competition in business means we have to provide a better product or service, or come in at a lower price point. We absolutely cannot share resources or customers and sometimes businesses find it necessary to steal, cheat, spy, and deceive in order to cut down their competition and win the game.

In one respect, this way of thinking and behaving is logical. We are built to survive, and our brains are wired to overcome that which threatens our life and livelihood. Just turn on a nature show to see how brutal competition in the wild can be.

Different Is Better

As in every other area of impact, it is imperative that social impact businesses operate with different perspectives and rules. If we are going to maintain integrity and live up to our labels of "ethical" and "conscious," obtaining the upper hand at any cost is no longer an acceptable way of operating. And as with the other seeds, it's not simply about "doing the right thing" for its own sake either; it's about the success of our long-term goals. As conscious leaders, the way we choose to view and treat our competitors requires a decision to zoom out and look at the larger picture.

At La Terza, we dream of a day when all coffee bought and sold not only in Cincinnati but also all around the world is sourced ethically and sustainably. As it stands now, the fact that our coffee is sourced ethically is something that sets us apart from some of our competition. It's a selling point and a unique offer. In an ideal world, however, this would be a standard way of operating. That means that one of our goals is eventually to rid ourselves of one of our primary competitive advantages. This long-term goal will lead to significantly more competition for us.

It seems scary—counterintuitive, even—to put the long-term success of our business at risk like that. But, if I zoom out and look at the bigger picture, I see that working with my rivals and embracing healthy, collaborative competition is essential to move the entire industry toward a more sustainable and equitable future.

I believe that the specialty coffee industry, with its rising popularity and shared goals of ethical sourcing, has a unique opportunity currently. Not only could we keep raising the bar and influencing how all coffee is traded, but I think we could be an industry that sets a new standard for global trade and ethical sourcing. Coffee is already such an internationally consumed product. It's grown all over the world and consumed distinctively in many different cultures. It's a product that connects us all together. If the industry continues to influence more people to buy in an ethical manner and begin to include even lower-quality coffees, opportunities to share learning with completely different sectors of business will open as well.

Iron Sharpens Iron

My family and I recently took a trip to a remote part of Michigan's Upper Peninsula, where we enjoy spending time on the underrated beaches of Lake Superior. You might consider my wife and me amateur foodies; we're always curious to check out the local restaurants, breweries, and coffee shops whenever we're away from home. The food we found was tasty, but it lacked a certain zest. The beer was good, but not great. The coffee was a bit watered down—although I admit that my standards in the coffee arena have become nearly unsurpassable at this point. As we kept sampling the different eats the area had to offer, I noticed that the overall quality wasn't the same as back home. I could tell that the restaurant owners, chefs, and artisans were passionate about their craft, but when I compared the entire food and drink landscape to the city, something was missing. When I later mulled this over, I theorized that the mediocre food and drink scene was perhaps due to a lack of competition. Being somewhat isolated from other cities and large towns, there was little around the makers on the peninsula to compare themselves to, and therefore, there was less opportunity to improve their products. Now, I'm not trying to be a food and drink snob. Someone from San Francisco or New York City might come to Cincinnati and say the same thing about us. And they may be right to do so: the competition in big cities is fiercer, so the standard, and therefore the quality, tends to be higher. My point is simply that an environment filled with healthy competition makes us better; it forces us to become the very best we can be.

There's a biblical proverb you've probably heard that speaks to how two entities can mutually benefit one another: "As iron sharpens iron, so one person sharpens another." As two blades are rubbed against each other, they are both simultaneously made sharper and more efficient. While this verse is often used as a commentary on friendship, I believe it can just as easily apply to competitors. Competition does not simply threaten our business; it provides invaluable opportunity for it. Competition pushes us forward, challenging us to innovate and provide better products and services to our customers. In order to create and sustain the best companies possible, we need competition.

Take a look at the diamond industry as an example. The monopoly-controlled diamond trade is notorious for being fraught with injustices, from child labor to environmental destruction to the financing of tragic wars, as was depicted in the popular 2006 film *Blood Diamond*. Not only that, but through incredibly successful marketing campaigns—"A diamond is forever"—the industry has convinced consumers that a diamond marked up as much as 200 to 350 percent is a necessity for proving one's love.

In the past five years, however, the diamond industry has been shaken up by direct-to-consumer lab-grown diamond companies like Clean Origin. Lab-grown diamonds provide a win-win solution for virtually every problem that traditionally mined diamonds present: they don't have to be mined and therefore present significantly less opportunity for human exploitation; the environmental impact is much smaller; and customers can buy them for just a fraction of the price of traditional diamonds. And yes: they are real diamonds! Even though they're made in a lab instead of in the ground, lab-grown diamonds are identical in their chemical makeup and physical properties; only a seasoned expert with a microscope would be able to tell the difference between an earth-mined and lab-grown diamond.

When Clean Origin burst onto the scene in the late 2010s alongside a few other lab-grown diamond companies, they brought a competitive edge that the large diamond brands had never had to deal with before. Diamonds that could be guaranteed to be ethical, sustainable, and more affordable? Of course, customers are interested! It didn't take long for big brands like James Allen, Jared, Zales, and Blue Nile to start offering lab-created diamonds as well. These big names have to keep up, and in doing so, their companies—and the entire industry—is moved toward a brighter and more sustainable future.

We see examples like this across all kinds of sectors. For example, one could argue that the rise in popularity of craft beer in America—from 5 percent of the market in 2010 to 13.6 percent in 2019—is what led the beer behemoth Budweiser to become the first US beer brand to list its ingredients on the side of its can. Budweiser wanted to appeal to the more health-conscious consumer who would normally choose a craft brew. Other huge brands joined in, even leading to a lawsuit resulting from an ad campaign about the use of corn syrup. In short: the rise of craft breweries caused the big guys to start changing their ways, leading the entire market to increase its transparency and put more attention on cleaner ingredients.

Competitive Collaboration

It's not only through free-market competition that we can change industries, but also through intentional collaboration with our competitors. In the story at the beginning of this section, it was my experience at SCA—a collaborative alliance of competitors—that refueled my spirit. In the apparel industry, you'll find similar groups, such as the Alliance for Responsible Denim as well as the Zero Discharge of Hazardous Chemicals (ZDHC), a network that includes Adidas, H&M, Nike, and others. Here are some other examples of competitors coming together for a common goal:

In 2019, two competing sustainable fashion brands, Nisolo and ABLE, joined together to create the Lowest Wage Campaign in an attempt to pressure larger brands to increase wage transparency for garment workers.

Samsung supplies the OLED screens and memory chips for their largest competitor, Apple, ensuring the mutual success of the two brands.

Until it fizzled out in 2017, the "Wintel" alliance between Intel and Microsoft was a successful, decades-long partnership that played an instrumental role in bringing personal computers into homes and offices across the globe.

Why would these competing brands choose to work together? In addition to the big picture reasons we discussed above, there are many other motivations that might lead competing companies to collaborate. Brands may want to enter into a partnership in order to get in front of a new audience, to amplify branding and PR, to expand their network, or perhaps simply to freshen things up with new content.

One of my favorite stories that I've recently read was about Burger King's "Day Without Whopper" initiative. In many countries, McDonald's has an annual "McHappy Day" on which proceeds of their Big Mac sandwich go to support the Ronald McDonald House, helping the families of kids with cancer. On November 10, 2017, all 101 Burger King locations in Argentina decided to get involved and did not offer their Whopper to customers. Instead, they pointed people to the nearest McDonald's to purchase a Big Mac. This initiative helped McDonald's sell 73,437 more Big Macs than the previous year, setting a record for McHappy Day in Argentina. I'm sure this was also a very calculated campaign by Burger King, and that any sales lost were made up in the following months with good PR. They even received international attention on social media platforms, which is how I found out about it. That being said, it feels good to cling to a childlike innocence, even if just for a moment, and realize that it's possible to support each other in order to have a deeper impact.

You never know what might come out of a relationship with a competitor. La Terza once helped one of our biggest competitors by brewing coffee for a large event for which they needed more equipment and knowledgeable hands. Just a few short months after the event, when that competitor didn't have the capacity to service a potential client, they referred the account to us instead. By offering a helping hand to our competitor, our business grew.

But What About When Things Don't Work Out?

Of course, there are times when things just don't work out. This doesn't mean that we should avoid finding ways for collaborative competition. As in a marriage, innovation through collaboration can be beautiful to witness. It takes a lot of work, it can bring out the best in us, and it can help us bring things to the world that we wouldn't be able to do on our own. It's risky to put yourself out there and to be vulnerable, but that risk can bring an amazing reward.

When deciding which competitors to collaborate with, it's important to choose wisely and move slowly. There is a healthy amount of vulnerability involved in working with your rivals, but it's best not to leave yourself and your business too vulnerable. The competitor I brewed coffee for? We had already built a working relationship. The brand's owners and I had had countless conversations before that—about the industry, the city, our personal lives. There were numerous small interactions that added up to a certain level of trust between us. However, La Terza has a different direct competitor with whom I would be much more hesitant to work. I've seen multiple yellow and red flags over the years, which have led me to put my guard up with this specific company. I don't have ill will toward the business, but I would think twice, maybe even three times, before partnering with them on something. After all, it's not just myself that I need to protect, but also my employees, investors, coffee farmers, and customers.

So, use discretion if and when you choose to enter a partnership with one or more of your competitors. It will be important to take your time and receive counsel from others you trust. You will also likely want to consider signing a nondisclosure agreement or other type of relevant written contract. If your team members will be involved in the collaboration, you will need to make sure they are aware of any areas that are off limits when talking with someone from the competing company, which might include confidential information like sales strategies or pricing information. Of course, we all want to give one another the benefit of the doubt, but unfortunately, conflicts do happen, so it's important to implement protective measures.

Creating healthy boundaries like these can protect you from a difficult separation, but sometimes this will be necessary. While I know I speak from an ideological perspective, my hope would be that if two social enterprises made an agreement to work on something together they would also do their best to end an arrangement in the best of ways and continue to ask, "How do I treat this organization the way I'd want to be treated?"

Again, think of healthy divorces where the parents still respect each other but realize that they do not work well as a couple. In this scenario, if they have children together, they still work together in sharing the parenting responsibilities. A healthy divorce in a business collaboration would look like protecting the social impact elements of the idea. It would celebrate each other's customers and future successes. In the end, each organization would still go back to what makes them unique and finding their specific place in the market.

Is There Enough for Everyone?

Sometimes, a healthy relationship with one's competition requires a mindset shift. It's easy to think that there isn't enough to go around: enough customers, enough money, enough accounts, enough resources. But is this really true? Sometimes, perhaps. But most of the time, I don't believe it is. There are nearly eight billion people in the world—all potential customers, and nearly forty trillion dollars in circulation—not including investments, derivatives, cryptocurrencies, etc. Ideas and creative energy are unlimited. I believe that most of the time, there is enough to go around, and that the fear, hoarding, and closed-mindedness that comes from a scarcity mindset is not helpful to our growth as individuals or our companies. So, the next time you find yourself feeling envious or anxious about your competition, try asking yourself: "Is there enough for everyone?" You'll probably find that the answer is yes.

PLANT

As we begin to think about our interactions with our business competitors, a good place to begin is to unpack how we are conditioned to compare ourselves to others on a personal level. I'm reminded of the phrase, "Comparison is the thief of joy." This wise proverb is a helpful truth to reflect on as we think of our interactions with our competitors. It seems that one of the aspects of the human experience is to always compare ourselves to one another. This does not serve us. When I find myself sad or depressed and I take a moment to reflect on why I have those feelings, I often realize that comparison is playing a part. I can easily get caught in a trap of seeing the success that others have and question why I am not reaping similar accolades. The harsh reality is that I'll never be the best or biggest at fill in the blank. None of us will. Even people who are best in the world at something are only the best at it temporarily. The most beautiful, athletic, smart, and wealthiest people will always have their records broken. There of course is value in comparing ourselves to grow and get better. Healthy comparison can help us be the best versions of ourselves, too. But to allow oneself to consistently compare who we are to others can be a negative, fleeting game with little reward.

Social media plays a significant role in how we see ourselves and others. And if you're like me, you have a love/hate relationship with it. On the positive side, it has allowed me to stay connected with old friends. It has even helped me to make new friends, finding people who are similar to me. The power of social media to share best practices and encouragement is one of the main reasons I think we are seeing this new social business model gain so much momentum. But with all of that said, one of the negatives of social media platforms is that we too easily compare ourselves with others. And to build on that, social media posts are often crafted to present the best versions of people and businesses. Think about the posts we often see about friends having the best vacations and meals or sharing a new look. There's nothing wrong with that—it's good to present what makes us happy and what gives us self-worth. We just have to realize that it's not the complete picture either. It's rarer to find authentic posts about dirty kitchens, sad days, and quite frankly, real life-moments. Again, I'm not saying that we should necessarily be airing our dirty laundry for the world to see. But we should also acknowledge that when we compare ourselves to others through social media, they are not complete or healthy comparisons.

One additional side note: When I find myself stuck in a negative rut of comparison, I also have found that I only compare myself to those who have more than I do. It takes a conscious effort to look at others and see how much you have compared to those who have less. I forget that compared to the rest of humanity past and present, I have so many privileges. I am in the top 98 percent of the world's wealthiest people; I have access to incredible resources and opportunities; I have eaten food better than kings throughout human history; and I carry a supercomputer in my pocket that gives me immediate access to communication and information. When I do compare, it's important for me to remember that I am one of the luckiest people who has ever lived.

WATER

One of my favorite business books is *From Good to Great*, by Jim Collins. The book compares eleven of the most successful publicly traded companies and tries to ascertain what they hold in common. One chapter talks about a shared trait it calls the "hedgehog concept," a name borrowed from one of Aesop's fables. The story is that when the hedgehog and fox interact, the fox looks like the clear winner. He's a fast, cunning, and attractive creature, able to do many things well. The hedgehog, is . . . well, just a hedgehog. He's not any of those things and seemingly should struggle against the fox. But what the hedgehog can do is roll up into a ball to protect itself, which he does really well. So when the fox and hedgehog engage, the fox gets frustrated and the hedgehog wins—every time. The singularly focused hedgehog is victorious.

In their studies of each of these companies, Jim Collins and his researchers found that the businesses in their case studies shared a laser-like focus when answering three questions: 1) What drives your passion? 2) What can you do better than anyone else? And 3) How do you measure your success? They often did not have as many resources as their competition, but they each saw significant growth as they answered these three questions.

As I have tried to answer these three questions in building my business, I have seen how the answers set me apart from my competition. They have helped me to focus solely on what I care about the most and have given me a path with clearly defined differences about who I am compared to coffee businesses in my area. Beyond that, these answers have helped me care significantly less about who my competitors are and what they are working on. It's not that I don't care at all, or that sometimes I'm not envious to see others' successes, but at this point, I've realized that what someone else is doing hardly matters. I know what we do well, what we are passionate about and how we define our success, and that's all that we need to be concerned with as we build our brand and interact with our customer base.

The answers to these questions have also helped me to realize exactly who my customers are. Coffee is consistently one of the most consumed beverages in the US, so there are plenty of customers available. This also means it can be hard to differentiate who exactly your customers are, because the answer cannot be all of them. Our focus has not only helped us to create targeted marketing campaigns, innovate new products, and conserve our resources, but it has also helped our team's culture by not getting trapped in the emotionally draining comparison game that is so easy to get sucked into. We have found our lane and we're really good at what we do.

Of course, not every industry offers such a large opportunity. Many businesses serve niche markets where there might not be very many customers. In this case, referring back to the studies of Jim Collins and his team is a helpful starting point. The more defined the answers to each of the questions he poses, the more success you'll likely see. And as to viewing your competitor as someone you want to treat like yourself, these questions can help you keep your focus on your work alone—defining what you do better than anyone else. The more we allow our minds to think in this framework, the less we view our competitors in negative ways.

GROW

As we talk about the small steps that each of these seeds requires, taking steps in the competition seed can be some of the hardest and most uncomfortable. I know that it has been for me, and I still wrestle with it. I can share with you some starting ideas of a few practical actions that can begin to lead you down this path. I promise you, it's worth it.

One of the easiest places to begin is to simply not talk about other companies with other people. Taking this into practice means that in our communication, we are not comparing ourselves to anyone else. Our perspectives about what we see from our competitors is likely limited anyway, so what's the point? When I have been asked by others about a competitor, I have learned to say, "I don't know about them really, I just know that we. . . ." It's much easier to stay in your area of expertise—YOU—than it is to presume and share information you're not versed in.

Another great way to begin putting this into practice is to meet with other people in your field from different geographical areas. This could look like seeking out a similar business when you're traveling, or maybe going to a convention in your industry to make connections with other attendees. Once, visiting a larger city, a connection of a friend arranged a behind-the-scenes tour of another coffee roasterie for me. It was a great experience, where I was able to learn a few new tricks on how we could better our business, while also sharing a few tricks that could help them. Honestly, it was such a breath of fresh air to be able to talk freely about our businesses without needing to be overly protective.

As you start to become more comfortable in these conversations, you can think of things like meeting with a competitor for coffee or lunch. Maybe there are safe opportunities at local networking industry events. Maybe with the help of your competition, you could form an alliance or plan a themed event. Seeking out a competitor in the same industry but with a clearly different clientele is another way to think about collaboration opportunities. Of course, you want to guard and protect your own interests, so small steps and holding to what you feel safe and comfortable with are important. But setting up space to meet others in your industry helps to humanize everyone, and you're able to see your competitors as people, too—especially when they might also be a socially minded business. The possibilities of a positive competitive community can lead to amazing collaborations and innovation, and they can truly build and energize an entirely new customer base and be the tide that raises everyone up, including you.

Environment
Rethinking the Costs and Benefits of Going Green

The Journey of Going Green

Soon after I began my work with La Terza, our local energy company called to set up an energy checkup appointment. They would come in and evaluate our space, looking for ways to help us use less energy and save money. I was intrigued, and while I assumed it was also a sales call, I set up a time for the evaluation.

This was also around the time that each of these seeds was becoming clear to me in our business relationships. And while the environment wasn't a specific group of people, it felt like it was in fact its own area of impact. After all, the entire human population shares this beautiful planet, so caring for the environment does affect people. Also, when thinking about organizations—and especially in corporate America—initiatives for lowering environmental impact were becoming more common.

We at La Terza were selling our coffee in compostable packaging, but I was excited to learn whether there were other ways to have a better environmental impact. The energy report came in, and it was true that we could save money and lower our electric usage. By converting from standard fluorescent lighting to new LED fixtures, we could save about one thousand dollars per year. Unfortunately, this would cost us about five thousand dollars, and we were already one year into a five-year lease of our space. Increasing our net positive environmental impact was a priority, but financially speaking, and because we didn't own the building we were leasing, we would save around four thousand dollars over four years by spending five thousand dollars up front.

At this moment in our company's history, we were still trying to grow our business by bootstrapping and without outside investment. We had just purchased new branded shirts from Joyya, increasing social impact within our supply chain. While this purchase didn't cost much more than conventional shirts, they were still an investment that would take some time to yield a financial return. This was also a time when I wasn't paying myself for my work. It was certainly what I signed up for, but spending a significant amount of money to improve our environmental impact and prioritizing that over my financial needs was not an option.

I was saddened by the realization that we couldn't do anything at that time. However, this was the first time I realized that we didn't have to take such a huge leap all at once to improve our impact. We couldn't make this change, but it did make me ask the question, "Is there anything else that we can do?"

I was proud of our compostable packaging, but when I asked this question, I realized that we weren't doing something even more basic—recycling. We had plenty of items that could be recycled—junk mail, boxes, and even the cups and lids we used to serve coffee. We did recycle some things at a nearby drop-off site, but because it was not convenient and took an organized effort to get there, too many items were thrown away. With that in mind, I inquired about the cost of a recycling dumpster, and for sixty dollars a month, we could have one. This was doable. And so we began a basic recycling program.

As our business grew, so did our efforts in working to minimize our environmental impact. Today we have been able to add a composting program as well, utilizing a service to send our coffee grounds to a local farm. The small step of adding a recycling container was a catalyst for future projects, and it was the first moment that I realized the importance of taking whatever step forward we can, even if it's not where we want to be in the end.

Climate change is also not just about us individually. It has become a very serious issue and is way too big a problem for one individual or small business to even make a dent. Because of this, it frequently feels like we have much more control and influence over the other six seeds. For example, by taking just one practical action, we were able to improve the well-being of our employees in a big way. The same goes for competition: we can set up one meeting with a local competitor and quickly make a big stride in this category.

Sure, our team can set up a recycling program at the roasterie or switch to backyard compostable packaging—and I do believe those are great initiatives. But it does make me wonder, "Are they really going to move the needle toward a more sustainable and thriving future for our planet?" Even as La Terza takes what feel like big and intentional steps toward becoming greener and more sustainable, it can be hard to see that our initiatives are going to make any difference in solving our climate crisis against the global backdrop. I don't want to be cynical, but I share this with you because I know I'm not the only one who has a difficult time with this category. If you struggle to stay hopeful about the environment, you're definitely not alone.

However, it's important to remember that small steps can and do add up when it comes to environmental sustainability—when we all take them together. This reminds me of the ants and elephants analogy we talked about earlier. In that moment, we were talking about the power of small- and medium-size organizations compared to larger corporations, and that we have more influence than we realize. The same thinking can be applied to some of our world's greatest challenges.

For example, approximately eighty billion pounds of food waste is thrown away in the United States each year. For health and safety reasons, a certain amount of food waste will always be generated—although we can certainly decrease that number significantly. But what if instead of throwing that extra or expired food into a landfill where it can't decompose, we composted it instead? By doing this, we could generate healthy, nutrient-rich soil fertilizer that could be put to good use in a variety of ways, all while saving eighty billion pounds of trash from our landfills every single year. If we all do our own small part, it can add up to a big difference.

Rethinking the "Costs" and "Benefits" of Sustainability

There is a common assumption that being more eco-friendly means spending more money. We may automatically think that organic ingredients or environmentally responsible production practices cost more than conventional ones. While sometimes this is true, it is not always the case. The next time you have an opportunity to make an environmentally friendly choice for your business, I invite you to let go of your assumptions about costs and benefits. You might be surprised to discover that going green could save you money.

There will be times when certain eco-friendly changes you want to make will in fact cost more. But it is important to zoom out and look at the bigger picture and time frame. It could be that there will need to be an upfront initial investment that will see a financial return in the coming years, and that a short-term investment leads to long-term savings. But, that might not be true; or as in our exploration of upgrading lighting for La Terza, the long-term savings are minimal and too far into the future.

There are a number of factors to consider when it comes to environmental impact, and there may be additional benefits beyond dollars spent and saved. Going green can easily be tied to new marketing campaigns and product launches. So, even though there is an upfront cost, it could also be an opportunity to gain new customers. This may also be an area where healthy competition helps to move initiatives forward. The more coffee brands there are who use recyclable or compostable packaging, the more pressure there will be for other brands to follow suit.

When I talk about comparing short- and long-term costs, it's easy to frame them in segments of one to two years and comparing with segments of five to ten or even twenty years. But, when we are talking about climate, thinking about the far future, past ten to twenty years, also has to be considered. This is playing out in our coffee business today. As the world's temperature continues to climb, the yield of many coffee farms is negatively affected. Research on helping coffee plants become resilient to a warmer climate is actively being worked on, and farmers are trying to think of far future alternatives also, including planting new coffee trees in areas with higher elevation that are ultimately a little cooler.

Thinking through all these factors can help us more fully understand costs and benefits. What might seem to be a short-term cost may turn out to be a benefit down the line, and what might seem like a benefit in the short term could end up being a cost in the long run.

To help illustrate what I mean by this, let's look at an assignment that Michael Toffel, a professor of environmental management at Harvard Business School, gave his students in 2016. Students were assigned to:

> *"Choose a company or nonprofit organization whose operating model is likely to be significantly affected by climate change's physical manifestations and/or related regulation, including threats and opportunities associated with mitigation and/or adaptation."*

In other words: explore a specific example of what climate change is going to cost a company. Over nine hundred students chose an organization they were at least somewhat familiar with and then wrote a short article about the challenges their chosen company is likely to face—or is already facing—due to the climate crisis. One student, Nikhil Dewan, wrote about how water scarcity might impact Coca-Cola. Another student wrote about the situation of insurance companies now that severe natural disasters are becoming more frequent. In these examples, climate change is bad for business.

This brings us back to the idea of rethinking costs and benefits. Let's use the Coca-Cola example that Dewan introduced. In his report, Dewan wrote about water being the "lifeblood" of Coca-Cola's business: as of 2015, about two liters of water are used to produce one liter of Coke. So, in 2007 the company pledged to replenish all the water it uses globally by 2020. They actually met their goal early in 2016 by implementing about three hundred different community water projects that focused on rainwater harvesting, safe water access, and more. In this example, those community water projects might be considered a short-term cost for Coca-Cola—they cost money and resources to implement and manage. In the long run, however, water replenishment efforts are not only a benefit but a necessity. The business is nothing without water.

Now, let's look at a problem that Coca-Cola has yet to address, in which the short- and long-term costs and benefits are slightly less obvious: plastic pollution. One report published by the NGO Tearfund analyzed the plastic footprint of four large drink companies (Coca-Cola, PepsiCo, Nestlé, and Unilever) in six specific countries (China, India, the Philippines, Brazil, Mexico, and Nigeria). According to this report, "Coca-Cola creates the biggest plastic pollution footprint in the six countries. The drink giant creates 200,000 tonnes of plastic waste—or about 8 billion bottles—which is burned or dumped each year in the six countries: enough to cover thirty-three football pitches every day." The translation for Americans: Coca-Cola creates about 440,924,500 pounds of plastic waste—enough to cover over forty-four American football fields each day. This is becoming an increasingly serious global issue, with plastic pollution negatively affecting ocean ecosystems as well as human health.

Environmentally speaking, Coca-Cola would do well to transition from plastic to fully aluminum cans and bottles. Aluminum is infinitely and more easily recyclable, whereas most plastics can be recycled only a maximum of seven times, and usually must be mixed with virgin plastic in order to ensure quality and stability. Plastic is also a product of the fossil fuel industry, which is largely to blame for the climate crisis we're experiencing today. Additionally, plastic bottles contain potentially toxic chemicals like bisphenols, which can leach into your drink and may cause chronic health issues over time. That expiration date on your plastic water bottle? That's not for the water—it's for the bottle.

Here's the thing about plastic . . . it's cheap. It's cheaper and lighter weight than aluminum and is not currently subject to as many tariffs. Switching to all-aluminum containers would be a financial cost for Coca-Cola and would have little obvious benefit for their business in the short-term. While the company's future is entirely dependent on managing global water supplies, curbing plastic pollution is not a necessity for the company to stay afloat. At least, not yet.

My aim is not to be a prophet of doom, but for the purposes of this argument, let's fast forward to a world fifty or a hundred years into the future. In this hypothetical future, little to no intervention to restrict plastic pollution has been made by Coca-Cola or any other company or government. Our oceans, which supply up to 85 percent of the oxygen for the entire Earth, are almost entirely filled with plastic. Whole ecosystems are devastated, causing a downward spiral that quickly affects humans in many ways: our food supply, our jobs, our health, our homes, and ultimately, the very air we breathe. If this kind of negative environmental impact were to continue to go unchecked and something like oxygen becomes a scarce resource, it's hard to imagine a world where a company like Coca-Cola would even exist. With the volume of waste it currently produces, Coca-Cola could lead the way to rethinking all our long-term priorities. And the idea of transitioning away from plastic as a cost with little to no benefit for their business would be reframed as the beginning of a transition that would enable Coca-Cola to thrive for generations to come.

Now, I don't believe events will play out in the way I just described. I trust that human beings will come together, innovate, and solve our climate crisis before it's too late. My point is simply to challenge the way we usually think of costs and benefits when making decisions in business. We should strongly consider the long-term consequences (or costs) of our short-term strategies and choices. No business, regardless of size, will be able to survive the total devastation of life as we know it on Earth. Long-term financial sustainability and long-term environmental sustainability depend on each other.

To further illustrate this idea, allow me to use one's individual health as a representation of the Earth's health. In many ways, living a healthy lifestyle can require more short-term costs up front. Healthy, organic foods can sometimes— although not always—be more expensive; you might have to spend more time learning how to cook healthy recipes instead of eating at drive-through restaurants; and you may spend money on a gym membership.

In the long run, however, those short-term costs will lead to long-term benefits and savings. You are likely to have a higher quality of life as you age, stay more productive and open to new experiences, and you'll probably save a lot of money on health care costs over time. Although it may be cheaper to live a less healthy life in the short term, you are likely to pay the price later on.

When we apply these ideas to the Earth as a whole, the investments we make (or don't make) now in our environmental health are almost sure to return to us in the future. . . . The question is whether that return will be positive or negative.

Sustainability Is Good for the Bottom Line

Now that we've talked about how operating in an environmentally responsible way can pay off in the long run, what about the short term? After all, you've got bills to pay! Investors to answer to! Orders to fulfill! Well, I've got good news for you: Research shows that environmental sustainability is now crucial to businesses' bottom line in the short term, too. You don't have to wait until ten or twenty years in the future to see your return on investment. Here are a few reasons:

Embracing sustainability is a key to remaining competitive in the market. As we've discussed previously, an increasing number of consumers want companies to prioritize ethics and environmental responsibility in their products and services. If consumers are given the choice of two products of the same price and quality, most are more likely to choose the eco-friendlier version. Many (roughly 40 percent of consumers based on some studies) will choose the eco-friendly version even if it costs a little more. Here are some other recent statistics to help show you how important ethics and sustainability are to consumers:

- One 2018 study found that 52 percent of millennials, 48 percent of Gen Xers, and 35 percent of baby boomers "feel it's important that their values align with the brands they like."
- Reports such as Nielsen Insights suggest the majority (73 percent) of consumers would change their consumption habits to reduce their impact on the environment, and almost half (46 percent) would switch to environmentally friendly products.
- More than two-thirds of Americans consider sustainability when making a purchase and are willing to pay more for sustainable products.
- More than half of consumers said they would pay more for sustainable products designed to be reused or recycled, according to results of a survey from Accenture.
- According to a 2017 Cone Communications study, 63 percent of Americans want corporations to drive social and environmental change in the absence of government action. Additionally, 87 percent of American consumers will make a purchase because a company advocated for an issue they care about. The study also showed that 76 percent of Americans expect companies to take action against climate change.

Where consumers go, so do investors. Obviously, investors want to give their money to companies that customers are willing to trust and give their money to. That means that the above statistics affect investor choices as well. According to "The Investor Revolution," an article in the *Harvard Business Review*, "environmental, social, and governance (ESG) issues have traditionally been of secondary concern to investors. But in recent years, institutional investors and pension funds have grown too large to diversify away from systemic risks, forcing them to consider the environmental and social impact of their portfolios. Analysis of interviews with 70 executives in 43 global institutional investing firms suggests that ESG is now a priority for these leaders and that corporations will soon be held accountable by shareholders for their ESG performance."

Sustainability is good for PR. Over the past few decades, we've seen huge brands like Nike, Disney, and H&M deal with massive PR scandals due to leaked information about their use of dangerous sweatshops, huge amounts of textile waste, and other problems. These scandals are costly to a brand's reputation and bottom line.

You can actually save money. As mentioned above, there is a common misconception that operating more sustainably is always more expensive. Although there may certainly be instances where the more responsible choice may require more cash upfront, be careful not to assume this is always the case. Take your utility bill as an easy example. If you take steps to conserve energy at your office, not only does it decrease your carbon footprint, but it decreases your energy bill as well. Many governments offer tax credits and other types of savings for taking green initiatives.

Step Outside the Eco Box

Don't be afraid to get creative with your sustainable solutions. What problem could you solve that's specific to your industry or product? How could you innovate and do something that no one has done before? As an example, let's take a look at what one brewery did about those dangerous plastic six-pack rings you often used to find on cans.

Six-pack cans now usually have a fully recyclable plastic top, but I'm sure you know the plastic rings I'm talking about: you've probably seen heartbreaking photos or videos online of a turtle with a maimed shell, a bird with its neck stuck in a plastic loop, or the insides of a fish filled with plastic pieces. According to marine biologist Mark Tokulka, an estimated one million seabirds and one hundred thousand marine mammals and sea turtles become trapped in plastic or ingest plastic and die. Over the past few years, people began to cut the six-pack rings so animals would no longer get trapped in the loops, and although this was better, it still didn't solve the problem for the animals who eat the plastic thinking it's food.

Saltwater Brewery, a microbrewery in Delray Beach, Florida, decided to do something about this. Solving two problems at once, they created Edible Six Pack Rings, which are not only safe for marine life (they're completely biodegradable), but actually feed them at the same time. The Six Pack Rings are made from a blend of barley and wheat, which the Saltwater team obtains as a part of their brewing process. The Edible Six Pack Rings are just as durable as any type of plastic ring, so product quality isn't sacrificed in the slightest.

This was an environmentally responsible decision by the brand, but it also helped business, too. Based on the beach, Saltwater's primary target audience consists of surfers, fisherman, and people who love the sea. Sure, these fish-friendly rings might cost a little bit more for consumers (for now), but Saltwater's target audience doesn't mind paying a little bit more if it means saving some of the ocean life they care about. The Saltwater team and their customers hope that this innovation will challenge big beer companies to take steps in a more sustainable direction as well. If a larger portion of the beer industry adopted the Edible Six Pack Rings, it would effectively drive costs down, making this eco-friendly option more affordable for everyone—large and small drink companies alike.

Even as new recyclable plastic rings have become more mainstream, many are still thrown away or become part of the recycling loop of plastic that still has many negative environmental effects. Part of what I love about this idea is that these rings are pushing toward zero waste, made from spent grains from the brewing process, and are fully biodegradable.

The creativity of this solution should inspire us all! Sometimes solutions can be found in asking new or different questions. Instead of thinking only how to make a change from a destructive package, a new question was asked: "What could this be used for?" Is there a problem that your company or industry faces for which you could push the eco-envelope and look for a new solution?

The Case for Starting Early

You might be reading this and thinking, "I'll do this later." Trust me: I totally get that, and I've had to make that choice more than once myself. It can often be more logical to get your business off the ground and stabilized financially before taking any initiatives in the environmental category. And while that specific timeline will look different for each individual business, I encourage you to take steps sooner rather than later. It's usually much easier to start operating sustainably at the beginning and grow from there rather than set up operations in a certain way, only to redo it all once you've grown. In the long run, this will very likely be more expensive. Try to think about taking steps to scale your company and your environmental footprint at the same time. If not, you could be unintentionally setting yourself up for failure if you try to grow first and then change things later.

Take the huge fast fashion brand H&M as an example. Overall, the fast fashion industry is infamous for being incredibly unsustainable. It's extremely polluting in the production processes, wasteful in designing clothes that are easy to discard, and continually utilizes unsafe and unethical sweatshops for production. H&M has certainly played a role in this system, but in the past decade, the corporation seems to be trying to make some changes. It started a garment recycling program and began releasing an "H&M Conscious Collection" each year to incorporate more eco-friendly fabrics like TENCEL, organic cotton, and recycled polyester into its clothing. It pledged to use 100 percent recycled or sustainable materials by 2030. It drastically increased the transparency of its supply chains, even earning the top score in Fashion Revolution's 2020 fashion transparency index. For a twenty-six-billion-dollar company that operates more than three thousand stores in fifty-three countries and can launch brand new collections of clothing in as little as two weeks, changing the entirety of its operations to reflect true sustainability is no easy feat. The supply of recycled and/or organic fabrics available cannot cover the amount of clothing the brand produces, and their efforts to put safeguards in place to protect more than one hundred seventy-seven thousand employees require a major commitment. If we give the team at H&M the benefit of the doubt when it comes to their initiatives and believe they're working their very hardest, the truth is that within our current globalized systems, sustainability for large companies is like trying to turn the Titanic—it takes enormous amounts of time and effort.

What if the team at H&M worked differently from the start? If they used organic and recycled textiles from the very beginning, working only with conscious and transparent factories as they built their business, they would be able to scale more easily together with their vendors. I believe this is a major advantage that small businesses have. We can make strategic decisions early on—choosing suppliers, pricing products, and putting other environmentally conscious processes in place early to potentially save ourselves a huge headache later on.

Beware of Greenwashing

As you start to plant your sustainable seeds, there's one major thing to watch out for: greenwashing. This means that a company talks about its commitments to improving on or having a clean environmental impact without actually being green. It's easy to say you're working on something without really making any changes. Unfortunately, this is common. A recent anonymous survey conducted by the Harris Poll for Google Cloud found that while most CEOs and C Suite leaders around the world said sustainability was a priority, 58 percent admitted that their organizations were guilty of greenwashing. This number grew to a staggering 68 percent among leaders in the US. Clearly, this is an issue that needs to be addressed.

It's possible that intentions are in the right place—that people within organizations do want to make changes. But, for a variety of reasons including the lack of financial resources, there's no implementation. This is why transparency is so important when it comes to the way your business communicates its eco-friendly initiatives.

Sometimes greenwashing is quite straightforward and obvious. Other times, it's more nuanced and difficult to identify. For many consumers, it might require a good deal of research and practice to develop the skill of identifying possible greenwashing. Like most things in life, what is eco-friendly and what is not tends to be more complicated than it may appear at first glance. Let me give you an example.

Rayon fabric (also called viscose) appears at first glance to be very eco-friendly, and many apparel companies market it that way. It's made from bamboo, a natural, biodegradable resource that grows very quickly with little water. On the surface, this sounds like an amazing product! The problem, however, is that a lot of toxic chemicals are used to turn bamboo into a fabric—chemicals that are toxic to the earth and garment workers. Additionally, a lot of bamboo is sourced in a way that causes long-term damage to old-growth rainforests.

Now this is sounding a lot less eco-friendly. So, what is the answer? Very quickly, this becomes a complex question. It is difficult to say whether rayon fabric is eco-friendly or not. It's also hard to accuse companies that use it and call it "sustainable" as participating in greenwashing.

My point is simply to illustrate the nuance that often comes along with eco-friendly claims. I want to encourage business leaders like you to make this nuanced information available on your website. An apparel company that has decided to use rayon in some of their pieces may explain its pros and cons, concluding with language like, "Rayon is not perfect, but we have decided that it's currently a better option than polyester, which is a petroleum product and will never biodegrade. We are committed to making continual progress toward increased sustainability and regeneration." You can see how using this type of language can help to build trust with consumers while preventing greenwashing. It's honest, transparent, and points to the larger eco-conscious trajectory the company is on.

Greenwashing doesn't have to be intentionally evil either; it can happen by accident. A well-meaning social entrepreneur may not be aware of an environmental issue until it's too late. That's OK—it can then be an opportunity to learn, grow, and earn even more trust with your customers by owning up to your mistakes. This is all the more reason to prioritize transparency, choose your words wisely when communicating to your customers, and be clear about your long-term direction.

EXAMPLES OF GREENWASHING

I try to keep one saying in my mind when I'm thinking about my branding and the branding of the companies I purchase from: "We are all the heroes in our own stories." This usually translates into communicating only good things about who we are, and sometimes bending the truth to paint ourselves in the absolute best light. I'm not suggesting that we air our dirty laundry (we all have it), but there is also a line of being deceitful that we shouldn't cross. Here are some examples of greenwashing that we should avoid:

· Changing the branding of a product or logo to include the color green and/or images of nature to imply environmental responsibility without changing the product or service to become more eco-friendly.
· Overexaggerating the minimal positive impact, while neglecting the larger harmful effects. For example, a single-use water bottle company advertises that the bottles are "Recyclable!" Nothing has changed—the bottles used to be just as recyclable as they are now. They are not made from recycled content and it really does nothing to help impact our massive plastic pollution problem.
· Presenting information in a way that's very complex to the average consumer, leaving it difficult for them to verify.

- Labeling a good or service as "eco-friendly" or "sustainable" with little to no explanatory information. Customers should be able to readily access more information about a business's environmental responsibility on the company's website or elsewhere.
- Focusing on the material without any attention to the production process. Just because something is made with an eco-friendly material does not mean that the energy, chemicals, dyes, materials, and other resources used to manufacture the product are also environmentally responsible.
- Distracting customers from other issues. For example, a company may be very vocal about its give-back initiative and use it to claim that their product or brand is "ethical" or "socially conscious." All the while they leave their customers in the dark about how their products are produced, so there is no way of knowing if the humans and environment are treated well.
- Being vague. For example, the term "all natural" doesn't really mean anything. Arsenic is all natural—does that mean it's healthy?
- Giving products irrelevant labels. For example, next time you go to the grocery store, check out the labels on chicken and turkey. You'll probably find a few whose packaging says something like "hormone-free." In fact, the United States Department of Agriculture (USDA) prohibits the use of hormones in chicken, turkey, and other fowl by law. This labeling

is used to convince customers that the product is healthier than a competitor's, when their competitor doesn't use hormones in their products either because it's illegal.

- Labeling something as "organic," "fair trade," or "natural" when only a small portion of the product or ingredients fit those labels. For example, a chocolate bar that contains 20 percent organic cacao can hardly be characterized as truly "organic."
- Advertising "green projects" for PR purposes. For example, an oil company that advertises their oil-spill cleanup.
- And of course, the obvious: making completely false claims or claims that cannot be verified by any third-party source.

The Power of Small Businesses to Turn the Ship Around

When it comes to sustainability initiatives, we've seen it so many times: small- and medium-size businesses roll onto the scene with a higher quality, a more eco-friendly product at a competitive price point. So, consumers make the switch. They say goodbye to the huge corporations and start giving their money to the smaller company. Then what happens? The huge corporations are forced to change. And then, entire industries can be moved in a more sustainable direction. Small businesses do have the power to turn this ship around and steer us toward a brighter and more sustainable future for the next generation.

PLANT

One of my favorite things to do at La Terza is leading our roasting tour. On this tour, we invite people to learn the history of coffee, explain how the trees and coffee cherries are grown and cared for, and finally, we roast a batch of coffee so people can experience the whole process. During the tour, I show a picture of a typical coffee plantation in Guatemala. In this photo, there are endless rows of coffee trees, all about seven feet high. At this moment, I talk about how coffee is one of the most consumed products in the world, and then I ask the question, "How many roasted pounds of coffee does one tree produce each year?"

The starting answers of each tour group vary greatly, but most people give me a starting answer of ten—which I think is a pretty good guess. The actual answer is a surprising one pound. Of all the coffee facts I know, this has remained the most staggering in my mind. When you pause to think of the amount of coffee consumed, it's easy to also think that each tree would need to produce an abundance of cherries. But, when you hold all the cherries in your hand, you can see that one pound is an abundance.

After I ask this question, I refer back to the large photo of trees and explain that with my family, I make a pot of coffee every day, and we go through around one twelve-ounce bag of coffee per week. I assume this is about average for many coffee-drinking families, and the people on the tours often nod their heads in agreement. Then I point directly at the photo and say, "This means that my family represents thirty-nine trees in this photograph." This is a powerful moment, because it is a visual representation of the quantity of resources necessary to provide something that many people drink every day.

The point of this visualization is not to make anyone feel bad or guilty, rather to have them understand the weight of it all. Maybe this does mean we should consume less too, but again that is not necessarily the goal. Our hope is that we encourage people to savor more. Understanding how much energy it takes to bring a daily cup of coffee helps us add a mindfulness to our habit.

I'm sure the same practice applies to nearly everything we consume. The closer we can move to the source of the things we purchase, the more we realize the energy it takes to bring products to us. This awareness supports a fundamental shift in our thinking about the impact we all have on this planet. The Earth gives us life in so many ways, and learning a sense of gratitude helps us to make sure we reciprocate.

I think it's an uncomfortable realization that there are other costs we pay beyond money when things don't cost very much. What I mean is that when costs aren't a little painful, it's easy to become wasteful. Five-dollar shirts are easier to discard when they get stained rather than spending time to get the stain out. Discarding uneaten food from a fast-food restaurant while taking home leftovers from a gourmet bistro are both normal. It's human nature to treasure things that cost more.

Sometimes the low cost of some things in our lives isn't because of the quality, but rather the quantity in which they are produced. Take a sheet of paper, for instance. At the time of this writing, a ream of five hundred sheets of blank paper costs around eight dollars, meaning each sheet costs about a penny and a half. When something costs so little, it's easy to forget that there is still a high cost in the quantity in circulation. Thinking about paper, think of the amount of junk mail you still receive in your mailbox everyday. It's a lot!

I wonder if we could all learn to actively think more often about all the costs in the things we discard. When buying paper, you could think about the lumberjacks and how dangerous that job can be. You can think about the trees that give us what we need to share information with one another. On average, it takes twenty-four trees to make one ton of virgin, nonrecycled office paper. Another way to say it is that one tree produces about seventeen reams. So, when you purchase 30 percent post-consumer recycled paper, you help save approximately seven trees per ton, or twelve trees per ton when purchasing 50 percent post-consumer recycled paper. Besides the trees used, producing paper also significantly contributes to water and air pollution.

So, while throwing one piece of paper away has very little environmental impact, a better understanding of the costs associated with all the paper produced can help each of us realize that it all adds up.

WATER

The exercise of adding up all the costs for the products we consume immediately makes me a little discouraged, because it shows that we have so much work ahead to bring significant change. But I hope it helps you feel encouraged, too. The small things we do actually matter and make a difference. As we form our new personal habits, I hope we keep this in mind. Small individual actions like combining trips, limiting waste, increasing recycling, and consuming less while savoring more do make a difference.

We also have to realize that we are not going to be perfect in changing our habits. I think this is one of the reasons why this area can be so difficult. We can't make all the changes we need to make, so we become discouraged to undertake any. From forgetfulness to limited budgets, the range of reasons to why it's difficult to gain traction are numerous. But we can't let the days we don't do well in bettering our environmental impact keep us from starting again the next day.

It's also very true that we can't bring these changes alone. And maybe even more discouraging is that it is difficult to see the results. One of the best ways to create new habits both individually and with a team is to incorporate positive rewards. Think about how hard it is to make changes to your diet and exercise routine. One of the reasons it can be difficult to change our habits toward a healthier lifestyle is because the positive results—losing weight or building strength—don't show up for weeks, months, or even years. Over time, you start to feel better, and as you do, it gives you energy to keep working toward your goals. The results of the new habits about environmental impact we develop may never be seen. This is all the more reason to make a conscious effort to celebrate our small wins and successes.

This is one of the reasons I love celebrating Earth Day. By making a holiday out of gratitude for the planet, we can build up to it with events and parties. Imagine what it would be like if the office Earth Day celebration was similar to our office December holiday festivities! Maybe that's something we can all work toward. In the meantime, setting up small outdoor events like having meetings or lunches outside, or celebrating Arbor Day with everyone planting trees can be a way to bring more attention to creating new habits.

There is a power in learning about the complete costs of goods that can not only help us shape better actions and policies, but also help other people join and actively participate. The more, the merrier! Understanding something like how many trees it takes to produce paper helps to form new office policies about what gets printed and what stays in a digital format. The key with this environmental seed is that it will take a collective effort to make changes, and each of us can do our part to help the planet regain its health.

GROW

So, are you ready to get to work? Every seed requires a "one step at a time" mentality in order to make big progress, but I think that might be truest with the Environmental Seed. Your team might already be total pros when it comes to taking action for the Earth, or you might be starting from zero. No matter where you are today, just start there. To help you out, here is a starting list of fifty ideas that you can potentially take this week, month, or quarter. Some of them are super simple—like taking a work meeting outside to enjoy the fresh air—while others will require a little more time and effort to implement. Do what feels right for you and your team. After you've finished with your first step, plan which step you'll take next.

- Create a sustainability committee or appoint an "eco office manager" for your workplace. This person or team can spearhead initiatives and make sure progress stays on track. This could be a volunteer or paid position.
- Set up a recycling program at your place of business.
- Start a compost bin for food scraps and/or partner with a local farm and give them your scraps once a week, or as often as needed.
- Next time you run out of something made of paper, replace it with something recycled or reusable. Computer paper, pamphlets, business cards, towels—you can even get toilet paper that's made from recycled paper!
- Take a work meeting outside and enjoy the fresh air.
- As the light bulbs in your workplace burn out, replace them with energy efficient ones.
- Opt for healthier team lunches with minimal packaging.
- Plan a volunteer day for your team to clean up a park or plant some trees around your building.
- Perform a trash audit.
- Hire a zero-waste consultant to help you practically decrease the amount of waste your business produces.
- Unplug electronics at the end of the day or when they're not being used. (They still use energy when plugged in, even when powered off or asleep.) Installing power strips can help make this much more efficient.

- Gift employees with reusable water bottles and coffee mugs to use during their workday in place of single-use cups.
- Replace your office coffee with an organic, fair-trade version, and stay away from disposable single-serving cups (like K-Cups).
- Go paperless when possible. Use programs like HelloSign or DocuSign to sign and save contracts electronically and securely.
- Switch from desktops to laptops where possible. (They can use up to 80 percent less energy!)
- Encourage employees to cycle, carpool, or take public transportation to work. Consider making it into a game and offer rewards so it's more fun.
- When switching out appliances like refrigerators and machinery, choose energy efficient options.
- When switching out plumbing fixtures like toilets and sinks, choose low-flow options, which save water.
- Perform an energy consumption audit. Take note of all the different devices, machinery, appliances, etc., that are utilizing energy, and approximately how much.
- Move a few of your business meetings to video conferencing rather than driving or flying to meet in person.
- Switch to nontoxic, biodegradable cleaning products.
- When purchasing corporate merchandise like shirts, choose more eco-friendly options like organic cotton, hemp, or TENCEL.
- Decorate the workplace with indoor plants.
- Give your employees paid time off to vote.
- Do a plastics audit, taking note of how much plastic is used in your supply chain and at your place of work.
- Install a living wall in your building (see sagegreenlife.com).
- Calculate your business's carbon footprint by using a tool like Carbon Fund.

- Offset your business's carbon footprint by donating to an organization like Cool Effect.
- When replacing furniture, choose a more sustainable option, like reclaimed wood. Better yet, go for used or refurbished.
- Buy supplies locally whenever possible.
- Partner with a nonprofit organization to plant trees with a small portion of your profits. Eden Reforestation Projects and the Arbor Day Foundation are two great organizations, but there may be one local to you as well!
- Cut down on commuting emissions by allowing employees to work from home once a week or once a month.
- Call your energy company and request that they use renewable energy to power your office or workplace. It may not be possible yet in your area, but demanding companies move away from fossil fuels can be a powerful motivator for them.
- Ship products in as few shipments as possible and avoid overnight and next-day shipping when you can.
- Use recycled or refillable ink cartridges in printers and copy machines.
- Talk to a LEED Certification specialist to investigate how you can begin to transition your building to a LEED Certified one.
- Install occupancy sensors so the lights automatically turn off when no one is using them.
- Get air hand dryers in the bathrooms to eliminate paper towels.
- In general, abide by the Three R rule, in this order: reduce, reuse, recycle.
- Make your product Carbonfree Certified.
- Become a member of 1% for the Planet, committing to donating 1 percent of your profits to nonprofit environmental organizations.

- If you offer physical products to customers, investigate how you might be able to increase the circularity of one of those products. Could customers send the product back to be repaired and reused after they're finished with it? Could you recycle it into something new?
- Adopt a highway in your city.
- Make a plan to slowly transition your company vehicles to hybrid or electric.
- Set up a system to recycle things like toner cartridges and electronics, which are recycled differently than plastic and aluminum.
- Learn how to make the landscaping around your building more eco-friendly. Some ideas include using drop irrigation instead of conventional sprinklers or planting native, biodiverse, pollinator-friendly plants.
- Research whether your suppliers and vendors are also taking steps to increase their positive impact on the Earth. If they aren't, initiate a conversation with them to inspire them to begin taking steps alongside you. If they're unwilling, consider doing some research and switching to new suppliers.
- Go solar! Install solar panels on your building's roof or call your energy company to ask if renewable energy is available in your location.
- Rearrange your office so that the desk are close to windows. You'll be able to save energy on lighting and absorb some beneficial vitamin D from the sun.
- Celebrate each small action.

Self
True Sustainability Requires Self-Care

The Most Important Seed

For some reason—I choose to blame faulty genes for now—my blood pressure likes to be just a bit high. My doctors tell me it's nothing to be too concerned about at this time, but I do need to monitor it regularly, especially the older I get. I'm not against taking medicine if and when I need to, but as of right now, I deal with it the best I can through diet, exercise, and stress management.

One particularly stressful week, I was unable to get my blood pressure down to where it was supposed to be. I was eating healthy and exercising, but it wouldn't budge. So, when a friend called me about taking a long-overdue afternoon kayaking trip, I knew I had to say yes. I needed to get away and unplug—if only for a couple of hours.

The little river was mellow that day. The sun was shining but it wasn't too hot; the temperature was almost perfect. Since it was a weekday afternoon, my friend and I had the water to ourselves. I absolutely love kayaking, but I hadn't been in one for a couple of years. It's one of those things that always gets put off for something else, pushed down on the priority list when something "more important" comes along.

Something more important always comes up, doesn't it? That day, I sat on top of the water, my hands dipping in and out of the river, and let my lungs draw in all the fresh air around me. As I watched and listened to the sights and sounds of nature, I was reminded (as I usually am whenever I make time to be in the wilderness) about the cyclical nature of things. That in order to pour into others, I have to first fill up my own cup. In order to give, I must remember to rest.

So, that afternoon on the calm river, I filled up my cup. I left my phone in the car and truly unplugged. Even just a few hours without any notifications, completely inaccessible to anyone else, was exactly what I needed. When I got home that evening, out of curiosity, I took my blood pressure. After a week or two of trying and failing to get it to budge, I was surprised to see the numbers on the little monitor's screen: 110/70—below average!

I returned to work the next day with renewed energy, ready to take on the day and work hard toward La Terza's goals. This experience helped me clearly see and understand the links between self-care, business success, and making lasting positive social impacts and just how important self-care is to both me and my work. Most of the time, however, it's not so obvious. I constantly fall into the belief that self-care isn't important, or that my to-do list or my mission should always take precedence over my personal well-being. I know I'm not the only one who gets caught in this cycle. I now find myself constantly reminded that if I am going to make a difference in each of the six other seeds, I have to regularly come back and make sure I am caring for all aspects of my health. Indeed, it is the most important thing that I can do.

I once heard a presentation about trauma and the speaker said something I've heard before, that "hurt people hurt people." There is a lot of truth and depth in that little phrase. But I think the opposite is true, too. That if I want to help people become healthy, then I need to be doing the work for me to be healthy. I'll never achieve perfect health; we all have pain and trauma scars that we must wrestle with throughout our lives. But the more attention we pay to our own health, the more safe and genuine capacity we can have for helping those around us.

Subtraction by Addition

I think one of the biggest challenges about learning how to take better care of ourselves is that we all know the things we should be doing better. Self-care often tries to incorporate doing something new or different. Most often, we know what we need to do and logically are all about all the changes we want and need to make. We know that we should fill in the blank: eat healthier, exercise more, work less, drink less, et cetera. . . . We know that much of the work we need to do is setting time to prioritize what is most important to us.

We hate being told no. It's in our DNA. Have you ever told a child that they can't have a toy or candy bar? If so, you probably are remembering that moment was followed by some kind of temper tantrum. The kid's focus has now intensified on what they are not allowed to have and they can't stop thinking about it.

The thing is, we adults are no different. We have a better understanding of why we shouldn't have what we are craving and better self-control and a few more reasoning tools available to help us make better choices, but we also still really want that toy or piece of chocolate. This is why the marketing phrase "for a limited time" is so powerful. At some point, we'll have to be told "no, you can't buy this" and we don't want to be told no.

So, in regard to managing our own self-care, we all have our lists of the things we need to remove. But a better practice and a little bit of a mind hack is to focus on the things we need to add. For example, I know I need to eat less red meat. When I only focus on trying to cut that out of my diet, I don't make much progress. But, when I focus on increasing my vegetables and am browsing tasty recipes that are either all or mostly vegetarian, then I eat less red meat simply because I am full. Another example is that I work and breathe in the craft beverage world, and I really enjoy craft beer. I do my best to pay attention to how much water I need to drink a day, and when I am successful, I don't have to spend much energy on how much alcohol I shouldn't be consuming. By the time the day winds down and I reach for a beer, I am not that thirsty and therefore, drink less.

This can even happen relationally. When we focus on spending time with people who inspire and bring the best out of us, we surround ourselves with negativity less often. This is not to say that we can't ever hang out with people who need us more than we need them, or that we can't ever have chocolate or alcohol, or binge on mindless television for a day. The point is that our time and energies are not limitless. When we can focus on what we want to add to our lives, we naturally begin to remove the things that are not in our best interest.

What Really Is Self-Care, Anyway?

How do we define "self-care"? The term has become trendy over the past few years. Search the hashtag #selfcare on Instagram and you're sure to find photos of candle-lit bubble baths and wine, naps and Netflix binges. Although these things might be aspects of self-care, they don't encompass what true care for self looks like in a holistic, long-term, and sustainable way. True self-care means intentionally creating a life that you don't have to escape from with bubble baths and Netflix. It involves learning how to listen to your body and knowing when it needs to rest and when it needs to create. It entails developing supportive habits so that you can get quality sleep, eat healthy foods, spend time with loved ones, and live with gratitude.

The bubble baths and Netflix definition of self-care is not the only misconception I often observe among social entrepreneurs. Another common myth: that self-care is selfish. Most of the social impact business owners and employees I know are not doing their work first and foremost to make money or earn status—they're doing it to make a positive difference in their communities and in the world. Taking time and energy away from that goal to rest, play, and enjoy life feels like a selfish thing for many. After all, there will always be someone out there who could use our help. There will always be more work to be done and a greater impact to make. For those who always have this fact at the forefront of their mind, it can be an internal battle to let ourselves take time off. But the truth is, not resting (or playing) is unsustainable.

The word sustainability usually brings to mind one of two things: financially sustainable or environmentally sustainable. But true sustainability is even more holistic than either of those two dimensions alone. The Merriam-Webster dictionary defines the word "sustainable" as "of, relating to, or being a method of harvesting or using a resource so that the resource is not depleted or permanently damaged."

The resource referred to here can mean different things—money, natural resources, or personal energy. Yet so many people completely forget or neglect this aspect of sustainability. Many professionals working in the social enterprise space strongly advocate for things like responsible environmental stewardship as well as fair wages and working conditions for employees throughout their supply chain . . . and yet they overwork themselves and don't pay themselves fairly. At some point, we must acknowledge our hypocrisy. We can advocate safe working conditions in our supply chain and for our team members and not overwork ourselves. We can promote environmental sustainability while remembering that we are a resource that needs a sustainable life rhythm. We are, after all, part of the environment, too. True and lasting sustainability insists that we treat our personal energy levels with the same responsible intention that we do our financial and natural resources. True and lasting sustainability requires self-care.

The Epidemic of Stress and Overwork: Everyone Is Struggling

The difficulty of practicing self-care is not limited to social entrepreneurs. I'm surrounded by chronic overworkers, and we have a serious stress and burnout problem, both in the US and around the globe. The numbers below help illustrate this stress epidemic—but note that all these studies and statistics are from before 2020, when the COVID-19 pandemic added several more layers of stress and fear for many workers around the world. As we come out of the pandemic, we are seeing the effects of even more of our societal stresses in how we interact with one another, and it will take years to fully comprehend all of the trauma we collectively experienced in the time after March 2020.

- According to a Danish study, women who described work-related pressures as "a little too high" had a 25 percent increased risk of heart disease.
- In a 2012 survey, 75 percent of Chinese workers said their stress levels had increased since the previous year.
- A Harvard Medical School study showed that 96 percent of leaders said they felt burned out. Ninety six percent!
- Japan's culture of overwork is such a big problem that they have a word for "death from overwork": *karoshi*.

- In 2018, a study showed that Americans left seven hundred sixty-eight million vacation days unused.
- In 2014, Gallup estimated that the average work week is now forty-seven hours long for a full-time salaried worker.
- In 2012, one study found that 28 percent of North American employees polled rarely take a lunch break, 14 percent choose to do so from "time to time" and 39 percent break for lunch but stay at their desks.
- A 2016 survey found that 40 percent of office workers in the United States and Canada feel burned out.
- According to Gallup's 2017 "State of the Global Workplace" report, only 13 percent of employees reported being engaged at work.

We clearly have a serious problem. This problem isn't limited to one industry or sector—it seems to be an issue in corporate America as well as the start-up world, and in for-profit businesses, nonprofit organizations, and governmental agencies alike. Our constant "hustle" culture and idolizing of productivity is making us sick—physically, mentally, emotionally, and relationally.

The True Impact of Stress

The statistics above are not theoretical or abstract; they have real consequences for real individuals. It's important to understand the impact that prolonged stress can have so that we can truly grasp the importance of prioritizing self-care in our life and work. After all, most of us "know" on some level that stress isn't good for us, but our larger culture lacks an urgency about just how destructive it truly is. Research has shown that stress contributes to anywhere from 60 to 95 percent of all disease, and that stress contributes to the top six leading causes of death. To begin to understand why this is, let's take a look at the role that stress plays in our lives, and how that has changed over time.

Our bodies use stress as a means of survival. You've probably heard of the fight-or-flight response. In order to survive, animals (including humans) have to be able to sense danger, and so we developed in such a way that when our brains are alerted to a threat, they send signals to our bodies that create a chain reaction. Certain hormones like adrenaline and cortisol are released, which make it easier to fight back or run away by speeding up your heart rate to get more oxygen to your blood, increasing alertness, and giving you a burst of energy and strength. Not only that, but your digestion slows, your reproductive organs shut off (if you're running from danger you're clearly not in a place to care for offspring!), and blood flow is redirected away from the skin and extremities and driven instead to the heart and brain.

This process is extremely productive and effective; it's allowed us to survive and make an incredible amount of progress over the past several million years as we've evolved into Homo sapiens with a modern and high-tech society. The problem, however, is that we're still employing the same system we were using back when humans were cave people and the most advanced technology was the wheel. Back then, our exposure to stress may have been more extreme in some instances, but it was much less chronic. If you were being chased by a predator, your body's fight-or-flight response would jump into action, do its job; and then your body's hormones would return to their normal homeostasis.

In our modern-day world, however, it's as if we are being chased by predators all day, every day. We are constantly bombarded with work stress, traffic, endless to-do lists, busy schedules, unexpected problems, the relentless heartbreak of the global news, and so much more. Our bodies are meant to use their stress responses sparingly, so when we are in a chronic and prolonged state of stress, a whole host of potential issues can crop up. When one's parasympathetic nervous system (which controls the fight-or-flight response) is chronically activated, it means their adrenal glands are overworked, they've got too much cortisol coursing through their blood, and their hormones (which basically control everything) are all out of whack. In the short term, this can cause headaches and a depressed immune system, leading to more colds and flus. Over time, however, exposure to chronic stress can lead to more serious issues like:

- Clinical depression and/or anxiety
- Autoimmune disease
- Heart disease
- Hypo- or hyperthyroidism
- Obesity
- Diabetes
- Sexual dysfunction and/or infertility
- Ulcers
- Asthma
- Addiction
- GI problems (IBS, heartburn, constipation, GERD, etc.)
- Accelerated aging, including exacerbation of Alzheimer's and dementia
- among other diseases and conditions

That's a long list of serious illnesses, and it doesn't even include the relational conflicts and general unhappiness that can be a common result of chronic stress. It can be a difficult pill to swallow, but the truth is that everything we've discussed so far in this book only works if the entire operation is conscious and sustainable on a personal level, too. So, many social entrepreneurs start their companies overflowing with energy and inspiration, with stars in their eyes. They fully believe in what they're doing; they are passionate about their cause and ready to change the world. They're willing to work as hard as they need to—to bring their business babies to life and impact their communities in positive ways. But so many end up sacrificing themselves on the altar of their work and their causes. They stop sleeping eight hours a night. They stop cooking meals and eating healthy food, opting instead for whatever is quick, easy, and probably unhealthy. They relinquish time with their family and those closest to them. They don't exercise or meditate regularly, and they never stop to take a deep breath or enjoy nature. I am guilty of all of the above on a regular basis.

Of course, there are always sacrifices that need to be made for the sake of a dream, a cause, or a business. Late nights, unhealthy meals, and missed soccer games are inevitable at times but where do we draw the line? How do we keep ourselves from getting too out of balance and totally burnt out?

As social entrepreneurs, it's important for us to understand the real impact that being under constant, unmanaged pressure can have on the quality and length of our lives. After all, we cannot be effective leaders if we are sick. We cannot bring positive change to the world if we're physically or mentally burnt out. It's so easy to get caught up in the day-to-day hustle, quietly believing that the sacrifice of personal health is worth it because we're doing something good. But I urge you not to forget the bigger picture. Yes, you are doing good work, but at what cost? You only have one life and you deserve to enjoy it, even while you do your good work.

Compassion Fatigue

When talking to entrepreneurs who are interested in starting a social enterprise, I often try to point out that starting a traditional, for-profit business is really hard and many fail within a few short years; so starting a social enterprise with a new set of self-governing rules is even harder. I hope you've also come to realize through this book that it's easier than we realize to be socially engaged simply by taking small shifts in how we look at our work. But, that said, it is true that there is often an extra burden to carry when working for a business with social impact.

Many of us begin social enterprises because of a strong empathy with other people, usually people in the margins. This has its own emotional toll that we have to recognize and be careful with. Of course, we want to help as many people as we can. It's also possible to let ourselves carry the weight of helping people who have significant needs. We feel deeply; that means we also have to guard how much we feel and ask ourselves. I think a healthy question to ask is, how can we clock out of our passions?

We need to give ourselves permission to unplug. Even with all of these seeds, we need to give ourselves permission to fail as we work at getting better and give ourselves grace for not being perfect. It's not that we don't care or that we shouldn't strive to do the best we can all the time. Maybe you can get there! But I think caring is a muscle. We are constantly building it and trying to grow its capacity. And just like a muscle, it sometimes needs us to give it a chance to rest and restore itself.

It's OK to go on vacation. It's OK to buy products without thinking about where they come from. It's OK to indulge ourselves and remember that we don't have to be perfect. We are not supposed to do this on our own. We can't, even when we try. We can only do what we can do, with the tools that we have been given. You are one person with a limited amount of energy and resources, and all you can do is your part. It's not up to you to solve all the problems or save the world. Only when we come together we will be able to dramatically move the world into a more ethical, sustainable, and conscious future. The human collective needs you to be your best "you" and to play the role you were meant to play. This means you need to allow space to rest and restore yourself so that you can plug back in with a new energy that inspires the rest of us on our journeys.

Our Families Are an Extension of Ourselves

I began my journey of social entrepreneurship in my early twenties, I got married in my early thirties, and my two sons were born when I was in in my early forties. Because of this, I had a lot of flexibility to adjust my work schedule based on my personal needs and without the need to consider others in my personal life. Being a parent is one of the greatest gifts and joys, but it also is a wake-up call for how much others need from you.

Much of the work in social entrepreneurship requires a different level of emotional engagement. We are often trying to serve and help other people in our work and there is a passion for different causes we care deeply about. One of the common challenges that social entrepreneurs face is that we can sometimes empty our emotional energies in our service toward others, leaving very little for our families at home. If you are single or without children like I was, you have more room to give more of your emotional energy to other people. But, as life shifts and you let others into your intimate spaces, at least some emotional energy has to be protected for the people in your home.

A person's work, regardless of the impact that it has or the good that it can do, cannot take away from the time spent with their families. Of course, there are times when work can take someone away, and there's an importance of balance, too . . . in that your family also needs to see that our work is important and that sometimes it does take us away for an evening meeting or for a trip. But balance is the key. Social work does require us to identify our priorities and where we spend our time and emotional energies.

Plenty of workaholics in traditional corporate jobs face the same issues. But, as social entrepreneurs, I think we can find ourselves more susceptible to overcommitting and crossing our life's required boundaries. We like to serve, so it's very easy to say yes to the opportunities that come our way. There tends to be a pendulum for many of us as seasons of overcommitting and saying yes often is followed by seasons of pruning and saying no to regain a balance.

The problem for those of us who like to say yes is that for every yes, we are saying no to something else. Unfortunately, this "no" is passive and many of us don't realize that we are even saying it other than noticing that our plate gets too full too often. This was a truth that took me a long time to realize, and not until I had children of my own did I realize how much I needed to think before I said yes to opportunities coming my way. There is still a sacrifice of some kind when saying yes, and again, it's good to say yes to things that you care deeply about. It's important for our families to see that, too. But, those yeses now come with much more thought and intentionality.

Mindfulness and Meditation

Usually people's first thought about self-care centers around how to better incorporate mindfulness practices. While the topic of self-care is more about the full self, meditation and giving space for our minds is a great starting point. And as with all the previous seeds, this one requires baby steps as well. Unless you're already to the point of illness, it's probably unrealistic and perhaps even unhelpful to suggest that you completely overhaul your life to make room for more sustainable self-care. But you can start somewhere!

As we discussed, our body's stress response is meant to be used sparingly, when we are really in danger. That means that when our well-being is not being threatened, our body should return to a relaxed state. If you feel like you've been doing a poor job at managing stress and taking care of yourself, don't worry too much. The good news is that our bodies and minds are extremely adaptable and can even be self-healing when treated right.

Neuroplasticity is a fascinating concept, which explains how our brains can literally be "rewired." We can train (or retrain) our physiological minds so that we're able to deal with stressors in a different way. Throughout this book we have discussed how we can change the fundamental stories we believe about business and the way the world works. In the same way we might learn how to speak a new language or play a musical instrument, we can also learn how to be resilient—how to "bounce back" from stressors on a biological and subconscious level.

Mindfulness practices not only give you an opportunity to slow down your life for a few minutes, but meditation is scientifically proven to rewire the brain, giving you an increased ability to handle stress, control anxiety, improve sleep, enhance memory, and more. Meditation can have a snowball effect. When you spend time observing and settling your mind, the effects can leak out into every area of your life—including your business.

The buzz around mindfulness and meditation has become louder in the West over the past decade, which has led many people to try—and "fail"—to start a meditation practice. But you can't really fail at meditation. All you can do is practice. Start again. Observe without judgment. Now, I'm no meditation expert, and there are countless resources available to guide you. But, especially as you begin to add a mindfulness practice in your life, I can share a few tips that could potentially help if you have found yourself frustrated in the past:

Start simple. Don't try to sit still for an hour right off the bat. Start with five minutes, or even just one.

Take the pressure off. Stop trying so hard. Many people think that in order to "succeed" at meditating, you have to completely empty your mind and think about nothing. In fact, there are several types of meditation and mindfulness in which that is not the goal at all! Instead of trying so hard to "think about nothing," simply observe your thoughts as if they are floating by like clouds. Remember to give yourself unlimited grace and patience. Meditation is not meant to be something else that stresses you out.

Use guides. There are many apps and other resources out there that provide guided meditations and other educational content to help you build your practice. Don't be afraid to check out different resources, experimenting until you find a teacher, a method, or a format that works for you. Seek out what has helped others in your relational circle and use the tools that worked for them.

Find others to go on the self-care journey with you. Finding a partner can go a long way in helping you both hold each other accountable.

Get back on the horse. Almost everyone I know (myself included) has started a meditation habit, only to let it fall by the wayside when life gets hectic. That's OK! Just start again, letting any judgment toward yourself fall gently away. This is another opportunity to give yourself grace, patience, and care.

Realize that you don't have to be sitting still to be mindful. You can practice mindfulness no matter what you're doing, whether you're conducting a business meeting, washing the dishes, or playing with your kids. To be mindful essentially means to be consciously present, aware, and grounded in the moment.

In addition to practicing mindfulness and meditation, here are some other practical self-care baby steps to consider implementing into your life:

- Use exercise (cardio, weight training, yoga, dance) to blow off steam, detoxify your body of stressors, support your immune system, and keep your body's systems running smoothly.
- Eat a healthy diet of whole, unprocessed foods with lots of vegetables in order to give your body and mind the nutrients it needs to function properly and handle stress effectively.
- Drink lots of water.
- Spend time in nature—it's scientifically proven to decrease stress and increase health and happiness.
- Set and keep boundaries around your work. Do this by:
    - Taking time off to spend with your loved ones.
    - Putting tech boundaries in place, perhaps dedicating one day of the week or hour of the day to being "tech free."
    - Delegating tasks when possible, instead of putting everything on your own plate.
    - Saying "no" more often.
    - Seeing a therapist to help you work through relational and work-related stressors. Anyone and everyone can benefit from therapy! BetterHelp is a great resource to try out for confidential, online therapy.
    - Pick up a non-work-related hobby to enjoy, such as painting, knitting, hiking, or gardening.

For this week, what's just one thing you can do to incorporate more self-care and stress management into your life? It might be something as simple as drinking an extra glass of water each day. It could mean taking a two-week vacation from work. Or, maybe it's something in-between. Whatever feels right to you, the most important thing is to take it one baby step at a time.

PLANT

THE WHEEL OF LIFE

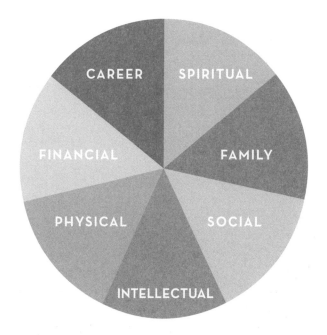

One of my favorite things to do is to meet one-on-one with a person who is looking for coaching in their career. This could be a high school or college student looking ahead as they try to figure out what they want to do or it can be someone older, looking for a career change. The people I have met with are often asking the same question, "How do I find purpose and fulfillment in my work?"

Several years ago I came across a tool that can help people answer this question, Zig Ziglar's Wheel of Life. The Wheel of Life has a long history, coming from the Buddhist tradition and representing a continuous cycle of existence: birth, life, and death. In Zig Ziglar's approach life is divided into seven key areas:

Career. Does my job give me meaning and fulfillment?

Financial. Do I earn enough money to meet my financial goals?

Family. Am I spending enough time with my family relationships?

Social. Am I investing in relationships outside of my family?

Intellectual. How am I investing in my mind and learning?

Physical. How am I taking care of my body?

Spiritual. Am I connecting to a higher being or collective human purpose?

The controlling idea of the Wheel of Life is that the areas of one's life are all interconnected and if just one area is not in balance, the circle is broken and everything is affected. It breaks down how we are doing in each of these areas and helps us see areas that we should prioritize differently.

As I have used this tool personally and in coaching others, I have removed spirituality from the circle. Not because it isn't important; rather I see spirituality in all of these areas. Think of it almost as a large umbrella that covers the entire circle. To be connecting in any of these areas is a spiritual act, so spirituality is not separate from the others. To take care of oneself, or to build into a relationship is deeply spiritual. An underlying theme of the Seven Seeds is that our work is deeply spiritual, meant to give us purpose and meaning.

When you look at the six remaining areas of life, they can be broken into three main areas, each with two sisters:

Self. How am I investing in my Intellectual and Physical well-being?

Others. How am I investing into my most intimate relationships of Family and close relationships, as well as my various Social circles?

Work. Do I have work that gives me a sense of purpose in my Career while also supporting my Financial needs? It is possible to make a lot of money but be miserable in your job. It is also possible to find fulfillment in your work but struggle to make ends meet. Is there a way to strike a balance?

As I have taught using this visualization, I also point to their interconnectedness. Maybe you have a job you love, that pays well; you have an amazing family and friend circle; and you are constantly curious about life and regularly finding ways to learn and sharpen your mind. But you don't leave space to take care of yourself physically. If this happens, you will likely live a shorter life or have physical challenges that have a profound effect on the other areas of life. This certainly has been me at different times in my life, and I am slowly learning how to find a better balance in my diet and exercise.

Similarly, if you are doing well in every area except creating space for time with your family, you will likely find yourself being isolated or even separating from your significant other and any children you might have. A person who quickly comes to mind who lived like this was Dr. Martin Luther King Jr. His work was obviously extremely important and necessary for our world, but it did come at a cost to his family relationships, including his wife and children.

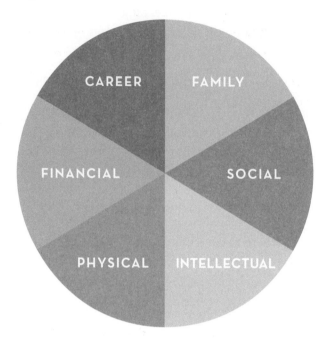

HOW I USE THIS TOOL

The point of the exercise is to help us better define and work toward our goals while also finding a life balance. Define what we mean by success in each of the areas, then work backward to lay out the steps needed. When I use this tool myself, I like to close my eyes and ask the question, "Where do I want to see myself in one, five, or ten years?" I want to create a picture in my imagination, so that I can begin with the end in mind. Once I have this picture in my head, I am then able to identify some of the steps needed on how to reach these goals.

There are a couple of things I need to point out. First, the goals you visualize need to be achievable. It's easy to dream of a life with limitless resources and success. That dream is probably not based in reality. For example, no matter how hard I try, I could never achieve a career goal of playing professional sports, even if that's something I wanted to do. So, when dreaming about how we define success, make sure it can actually be reached.

Second, the goals need to be balanced. To start, I encourage defining what success looks like in each of these areas one at a time before seeing how they relate to one another. After you do that, you will need to go back and see how each of the areas relate. For example, you may have a goal to save five million dollars in the next five years. Maybe this is achievable, but in order to reach this goal, most of us would have to make significant sacrifices in every area of the wheel. Are your relationships something you'd be willing to sacrifice in order to achieve this goal? Probably not. And even if you said yes, you might not be able to realize this goal.

Third, as we define our successes and what we hope for, we need to be completely honest with ourselves. If your goal is to have a large house with a Ferrari in the garage, then make sure you say that. These are your dreams, and when you write them out, it is not the time to be altruistic. Ask yourself what resonates most with you in each of these areas; why you want success to look a certain way; and why some dreams have a higher priority than others? These questions will help guide us to visualize what we really want to do with our lives.

Fourth, each area is fluid. They are not designed to be six equal pieces of a pie. Life looks different to all of us, and so does the way we define success in each of the areas. As I entered the workforce, I was happily single and did not have to devote much time into the Family piece of the circle. I still had relationships to nurture with my parents and siblings, and I would also put dating into this category, so I did spend some time here. But overall, this area didn't require a lot of my attention. Even when

I did get married, I didn't have children for several years. So, my Family attention was less than what it is today, which afforded me more time in the other areas for that season of life.

Finally, I find it helpful to personally revisit this on a regular basis. The only constant in life is that things are always changing, including our own goals and priorities. When I go through this exercise with someone, I write out my goals, too. This helps me to be very clear about what I hope to see in my life, as well as keep a record of past goals. It gives me a way to measure progress and even see how new priorities reveal themselves to me as I get older.

WATER

As we incorporate new goals in our lives, the next challenge will be to achieve them. Identifying your goals is a necessary and important step, but it can be much more difficult to change the habits needed to reach them. Most of us know the changes we need to make from a logical perspective. But the amygdala and the limbic system of our brain that control our emotional responses are a powerful force and can very easily take over our logical decision-making ability.

Changing our goals is also a challenge because it's always a long game. It takes time to reap the benefits of our new priorities, so it has to be approached like you're making a long-term investment in yourself. This is in part why we have stressed celebrating small wins in each of the Seven Seeds, but it is extra critical to embrace this principle in our own lives.

It's not that the small win will have that much of an impact, but when you see the sum of the small wins together, you can observe progress being made. This is why journaling is such a powerful practice. You can see over a long period of time how you are incorporating new habits and feel like you're making real change.

I've included this worksheet

Defining Success vs Setting Goals:

- DEFINING SUCCESS is beginning with the end in mind.
- SETTING GOALS is defining the achievable steps along the way.

Tips For This:

- Needs to be balanced.
- When defining success, also ask why.'

- Needs to be achievable
- It will take time and work, but it's still worth it!

How do you define success in each area?

CAREER

FINANCIAL

FAMILY

SOCIAL

PHYSICAL

INTELLECTUAL

Zig Ziglar's Wheel of Life

Everything is Spiritual!

Celebrating small wins also helps us slowly gain momentum. When we celebrate our wins, we are also helping to create a positive memory. And the more we start to take care of ourselves, the more we want to keep going. Self-care begets self-care. The more we begin to feel resourced, the more we start to get resources. By gaining traction, we can enable another important mindset shift: moving from what we know we need to do to habits that are simply nonnegotiable. The good habit is no longer something we know we should do, it has simply become a part of our life's rhythm.

Another major challenge is that we're incentivized and genuinely rewarded to choose things that take away from self-care. They give us a quick dopamine hit but are unsustainable forms of good feelings. Think of that piece of candy, a relaxing beverage, or even text alerts on our phones. They all make us feel good, so we want more of them. The problem is when they come in larger doses, they take away from our long-term goals. We certainly should enjoy these things in moderation, but we should put up guardrails for each. Sweet treats fill us up but provide little nutrition. Adult beverages dehydrate us. Texts connect us to people but also distract us from being present with people we might be with in that moment. As mentioned earlier in this section, focusing on what to add versus what to remove can help us to create new habits that last.

It can be surprisingly hard to be honest with ourselves. We very easily justify our behaviors and ignore the changes we should be working on. We ignore pinches—the little ways that our body is trying to tell us something. We either stop listening to our body completely, or find ways to medicate and drown out the noise. This is probably what I gained the most from when I made space for mindfulness practice. I stop to feel what my body is telling me. When I do this, I am shocked at how much information I am regularly ignoring. I find that different joints and muscles are hurting, or that I am dehydrated. These aren't large problems, which is why I can ignore them. But, then all of a sudden, I pull a muscle in my back and I can't get out of bed. It's like my body finally has had enough and forces me to listen in a loud voice because I haven't been paying attention to the quiet voice. Journaling, adding in a mindfulness practice, and finding a kind of accountability partner are huge ways to help bring awareness to the way we care for ourselves.

Finally, a practice that has been very powerful for me is to measure progress over a week or two instead of a day. When I set out a new goal but let a day go by without doing what I wanted to do, I feel like I've failed myself and it becomes very difficult to find motivation the next day. Just one day when I'm unsuccessful can derail how I feel about the days when I've had success. This makes me just want to give up. I have learned that it's better for me to look at days throughout the week. Maybe it just starts with one or two days of progress. Celebrate that. Soon, it might be three to four days and eventually you will have incorporated a new habit. Coming in with a beginner's mind is a key component to self-care. If you made a choice an hour ago that you regret, it's OK. Now is a great place to begin again.

GROW

So much of self-care requires creating more space for ourselves. For some of us, it would be good to reframe what success in our work life means and holding firm to forty-hour work weeks. Maybe we might even think about what less than forty hours looks like. A dear friend of mine who is absolutely brilliant used to work sixty to seventy hours a week. Several years ago, and in part because her body forced her to make some changes, she realized she needed to step back significantly from her work and she cut her time in half to thirty hours a week. As a result, she was able to reset so many aspects of her life. She played more, had more fun, was able to sleep well, and while she did work less, her brilliance was magnified. She was significantly better at her job, and she has come to realize that if she is to continue to thrive in her work and bring her best self to her company, she has to hold her time boundaries tightly.

This reminds me of a concept that my friend Maggie from the beginning of this book once taught me, and has stuck with me ever since. There is a phrase commonly used in sports, that we'll give it 110 percent. We all know that's impossible, right? The most we can give at any moment is 100 percent. And even then, the reality is that for us to function well, most weeks should be at something like 70 percent. Of course, there are times when we need to step up to meet a deadline or push through a project, but our work rhythms should be sustainable. Always being at 100 percent does not sustain us.

Think of a car that has a redline of seven thousand RPMs. We can drive on the highway in third gear, maxing out at the engine's 100 percent capacity, but none of us do that because we know it would significantly reduce the life of the car. Instead, we know that the engine is at its best when its humming along at 50%. We are the same. It's OK to push ourselves, and we need to do that sometimes. But what is our optimum capacity and how do we work from there the most often?

Our seven-day weeks seem to have a certain rhythm. Most of us work five days a week, have one day to work and catch up on all the miscellaneous things in our lives, and one day to rest and play. We can restore ourselves on the weekend and prepare for good work in the coming week. What if this restoration rhythm was expanded? If one day a week is for rest, then can one weekend a month be for rest also? Maybe we should also take time to rest one week per quarter. And I think going the other direction is helpful as well. Taking one hour a day for ourselves, and one minute per hour to pause and be mindful.

I recently came across the book *Sacred Rest* by Saundra Dalton-Smith, which talks about seven areas of rest—physical, mental, spiritual, emotional, sensory, social, creative—and how each area of rest plays a critical role in our overall health, happiness, relationships, creativity, and productivity. Naturally, I was drawn in because there were seven areas to think through.

(Just kidding—though there is something really fun about that number.) Here is a quick list of the seven types of rest and examples of each:

Physical rest: engaging in physical activities like taking a walk or exercising

Mental rest: setting time aside for quiet, silence, or meditation

Emotional rest: finding a safe place to process your thoughts and be your truest, authentic self

Spiritual rest: taking time to engage in spiritual practices and unplugging in a way that takes the focus off ourselves and puts it onto the larger universal collective

Social rest: actively engaging with other people who fill us up

Sensory rest: eliminating screens, sounds, and technology

Creative rest: engaging in a hobby and actively creating

Breaking down the seven areas of how to rest and rejuvenate helped me think about the different ways to rest and the intentionality required to engage with each type. I imagined what activities I enjoyed in each of these seven areas of rest and how they all gave their own unique feelings of restoration. This framework also helped me understand how some activities —like riding my bike—could require a lot of physical energy but also be restful. I also could quickly feel how imbalanced I was and that I had been neglecting some forms of rest.

The framework of the different types of rest, overlapping with new restoring rhythms hourly, daily, weekly, and quarterly, have given me a new framework on how to create more space for self-care. I am excited to be better at self-care, and I hope you are, too. The more we care for ourselves, the more we are able to care for others in our work.

PART THREE

Prepare Your Garden

Beautifully Angry

For a long time, the news seems like it has mostly been sharing all that is wrong with the world. Culture wars are at an all-time high and playing into the emotion of fear keeps us from even the desire to try to understand the perspectives of the other side. Rather than unpack the important issues at hand, each side has to try to one up the opposing view with its own shocking statements. We have lost the art of listening and it shows in how we interact with one another. News feeds are filled with images of our emotions reaching a boiling point over everyday life: road rage turning deadly, people needlessly yelling at referees, or physical fights breaking out because of disagreements over issues like mask mandates. Our fears and angers as a society have become misplaced.

The thing is, fear and anger are very good emotions. As an emotion, anger tells us when boundaries have been crossed. It can show us where injustices are and give us the passion to make real change. Fear is an emotion designed to protect us and keep us from harm's way. It is critical to our survival, both individually and for the human race. The question becomes, How can we better process these emotions and dive deeper into their roots. Asking the "why" questions—"Why are we angry?" and "Why are we afraid?"—can help us to better address the causes of our emotions rather than simply acting on emotional energy alone.

In the 2018 documentary *Won't You Be My Neighbor*, about the life of Fred Rogers, there was one quick moment toward the end of the movie when Fred's family was reflecting on how he was often driven by anger. They said that Fred would see something in our society that he saw as wrong—racism, war, and treating marginalized people differently—and he would use that anger to produce topics for his children's show. This moment helped me to realize that there can be a beauty in our anger when we use it to focus on important issues.

I have often found myself talking with high school and college students about what they wanted to do with their lives and what they would study, and a common question they wrestle with is, "What do I love to do?" It's a fantastic question and one I continue to wrestle with myself, but I think an equally important question to ask is "What do you see in this world that you hate?" To me, love and hate are two sides of the same coin. Each is an emotion of deep passion, and those passions can drive our vocational pursuits. Whatever your work is, there are the good days and the bad. In the hardest days, those passions can sustain us to keep moving forward. They can keep us focused on what matters most, how we can be more effective, and give us the fuel to keep fighting the good fight.

One day in July 2019 as I was reading the morning news, I saw an Associated Press photo taken by Julia De Luc of a father and his almost two-year-old daughter who had drowned trying to cross the Rio Grande at the US-Mexico border. Also at this time, a caravan of people from Central America had traveled to the border to try to gain entry into the United States, and the topic of immigration had become an extreme political topic. This photo of Oscar Alberto Martinez Ramirez and his daughter, Valeria, encapsulated the grim reality that many migrants were forced to choose between: extreme poverty and crime in Central America, or risking their lives —and often the lives of their families—for a chance for a better life in the United States.

This particular image was especially gut-wrenching for me because I had a son who was almost exactly the same age. I sat with the image struggling to understand how a father might risk everything, taking his child to swim across a river to safety. The only way I could try to describe how I felt was the mental scenario where you would find yourself in a burning building and if you stayed inside, you would be sure to die. But, if you jumped from a second-story window, you'd probably not survive, but at least you'd have a chance. I was heartbroken, feeling like a sense of basic humanity had been lost.

I continued my day, but my team noticed that I was dramatically different. Despite it being a pretty good day for business, I was pretty down instead of my being my normal cheerful, optimistic self. By midafternoon, my team manager pulled me aside to ask me what was wrong. Honestly, by then I had blocked the image from my mind and didn't associate my negative feelings with the photograph. It wasn't until she kept pressing to figure out what was bothering me that I realized the emotions of the photo were still sitting with me. As I described the image, she told me about an organization called Preemptive Love that was sending backpacks filled with basic supplies to the border to help with the crisis. The idea was that regardless of political perspective and beliefs about immigration, people could agree that everyone should have access to necessities like toilet paper, soap, and toothpaste.

I logged into their website preemptivelove.com, and for forty dollars was able to purchase a backpack of supplies and send them to the border. And, while I wish I could have sent a hundred backpacks, I did feel slightly better knowing that I was able to do something. While on their website, I noticed Preemptive Love also had a podcast called Love Anyway. One of the episodes was specifically about immigration, the border crisis, and the caravan of immigrants on the journey to the United States border. I was excited to listen to this episode on my drive home from work, as it might help me to continue to process all of my emotions.

The episode, titled "The Border Wall," featured an interview with Matt Malcom, an Army veteran who wanted a better understanding of the fear that surrounds the issues of immigration. He was curious to join the caravan and learn firsthand why people were desperately trying to come to the United States even while our immigration policies had moved toward near-zero tolerance. Some news outlets were reporting that the caravan was filled with rapists, murderers, and gang members intent on infiltrating the United States in an effort to bring additional violence to American communities.

Matt shared his experiences interacting with people in the caravan, and the story that impacted him the most was that of a mother of three—one son and two daughters —from Honduras. Her son was being recruited by the local gang and he did the right thing, refusing to join. In retaliation, the gang raped her older daughter. To escape this situation and the risk that her younger daughter would also be raped, she joined the caravan to do whatever she could to protect her family.

Listening on my drive home, in stop-and-go rush hour traffic, I can tell you exactly where I was when I heard this story. I burst into tears and started yelling, pounding my fist into the steering wheel. I was angry at a level I have rarely felt, and sick to my stomach about how immigration had become such a polarized issue that we had forgotten the humanity of our neighbors. In my opinion, regardless of the politics about who comes into our country—which admittedly is complicated—the basic requirement of treating others as human felt like it had been lost.

In the next few minutes, as my anger started to calm, I began to brainstorm about what I could do. I had to do something beyond buying a backpack of supplies. Then I suddenly I realized that I work in coffee and I have business relationships in Honduras. More than most people who might feel helpless about this situation, I was in a position to do something. We could highlight how sourcing coffee ethically in Honduras lifts people from poverty, keeping them from joining gangs or from being forced to make the difficult decision to try to come to the United States illegally. We were also in a position to help Preemptive Love raise money by helping them sell coffee. La Terza had a great online system already in place to ship coffee all over the country. Preemptive Love could simply add the product to their website and we could handle fulfilling all of the orders. And in addition to helping them raise money, we could show people a way to participate in a system that contributed to solving at least a part of the immigration problem, simply by making a choice about what coffee they purchase. Buying coffee from us, coffee from other roasters with similar procurement practices, even items like chocolate and fruit. When they are purchased with the idea of fair trade in mind, one can make a difference in the complex issue of immigration—and do so regardless of one's political leanings.

The next morning, we reached out to Preemptive Love with the idea: sell coffee on your website, take the profits minus our production and material costs, and we'll handle fulfilling the orders. It was a pretty easy decision for them—take all of the profits, we'll do all of the work—but it has turned into a long-term, mutually beneficial relationship that has lifted everyone involved. It turns out that they had been thinking about adding coffee to their website when we contacted them. For the rest of the year, we sold coffee to Preemptive Love at our cost and were able to help them raise over five thousand dollars to go toward border supplies.

We were able to share the story of our direct trade relationship with Katia Duke, helping her sell more coffee and providing more jobs. And as we moved into the following year, Preemptive Love transitioned to a new wholesale account with us where they could still benefit from most of the profits but we could sustain our business as well. Oh, and the customers who purchased from Preemptive Love—they loved the coffee! We heard so many comments about how they made the purchase to support the cause, but were delighted to find the coffee some of the best they had ever had. There were even comments from the Pacific Northwest (the coffee mecca of the US), where there are many specialty coffee roasters to choose from.

This story and all who benefited from it was born from my extreme anger caused by seeing a horrifying photo of a father and daughter, and listening in my car to the account of a scared mother. When I take a deeper dive into why I was so emotional, I realized that it was because I felt complete helplessness.

Perhaps that is where much of our misdirected anger in our culture is coming from . . . helplessness. When we feel like we're not able to do anything, it becomes very difficult to process our emotions without turning up the volume—both internally in how we feel as well as externally in our voice and actions. Metaphorically, we find ways to shout our emotions as loud as we can, trying to raise awareness of our pains and fears.

It has become a lesson learned that when anger builds inside my mind, I need to try to take a moment to pause and think about where the anger is coming from. I have to search deep within and ask myself whether the energy could be diverted to solving the problem rather than filling with rage. For me, it takes a new discipline and intentionality to apply this idea to my mindfulness practices and reminds me of why they're so important. On one hand, I realize that I am often helpless and that what I can do makes only a small impact. There is an acceptance to this that oddly gives me a sense of peace and calm. It's the idea that I don't have to carry the weight of the world on my shoulders, and that's a good thing. And then, with this sense of peace, there can also come a clarity. Because I don't have to think about the whole world, it gives me the space to focus on what I actually can do. Just as in the story above, once I gave myself a calm space to think about what I could do, I very quickly identified actions that not only helped others but also allowed me to process my own emotions in a very positive way.

For those working in social enterprises, I think it's a healthy habit to listen to your body when it wells up inside . . . noticing what causes your blood pressure to build and your fists to clench. The key from there is to do something productive about it. Don't let that anger go to waste, stay inside, or be spent in the wrong places. Find a way to use the anger you feel to make a positive impact in the world.

And as far as raising our collective voices in order to be heard, I think we need to keep going back to the image of the ants and the elephants. How can we share what makes us upset in a way that is a call for other ants with similar passions? Let's figure out what small step of impact we can take individually, and then collectively. From there, we need to find as many ants who are marching in the same direction. We can make a difference when we learn how to march together. Our collective actions will speak volumes without the need to raise our voices. Ants, by the way, are also pretty quiet.

As we begin to take actions, we need to do everything we can to listen intently to those we disagree with. Remember . . . two ears and one mouth. This will be scary and uncomfortable, and there will be times when this seems like it's not an option. But when we are championing a cause where not everyone agrees, we need to do our best to present a posture of curiosity to the other side, helping us to ask better questions around why they are passionate in causes we are against.

I bring this up because as I write this, our society is in the middle of some pretty heated culture wars. Local governments and school boards are responding to the talking points of the extreme sides, something that again, makes me feel helpless. I have many strong opinions about topics like Critical Race Theory, what it actually is, and how it should be taught in our school systems. But when I come in hot, I only raise the volume in the room. In contrast, when I come to the table to ask better "why" questions, like why someone is concerned about the issues and what they hope to accomplish, then an actual dialogue more possibly could take place and the potential to find common ground is much higher. Of course, listening and entering a conversation with curiosity takes a willing second party, which is why this won't always work. But by doing the work to create a safe place for someone to truly express their fears and concerns, we can have a better opportunity to bring changes to the subjects that so often divide us.

Embracing the Journey

To begin, think of some of the causes that you deeply care about. What stories overwhelm you with joy when you see humanity step up in the best ways? I can think of videos I've scrolled through on social media feeds in which someone rescues an animal that is caught in a fence; or when an athlete, sacrificing the chance of victory, stops to help an injured competitor finish in a selfless act of sportsmanship. These memories might inspire you to think of how you could help better care for animals or invest in kids' sports programs.

An equally important practice is to think about the things in this world that make you personally upset, angry, or feeling helpless. Immediately, I think of commercials I've seen that ask for money to help with some of our biggest needs like child hunger. When I see something like this, I get so angry because I have a hard time understanding how this issue exists in the world. Corrupt governments, misuse of resources, improper distribution, or an extreme misallocation of wealth—none of these, in my mind, are good enough excuses to allow our smallest people to suffer from hunger. Even in writing this paragraph, I can physically feel my body become tense and upset.

With that said, we have to remember: we can't take on the world alone. We have to recognize that we can all only do what we can do. For example, when I see that commercial, I also have to allow myself to become numb to it. No matter your financial situation, for all of us, our resources our limited.

For many people, while it's not a lot, twenty dollars a month is too big of a financial commitment to give to another organization. I would guess that many who want to give are likely supporting other causes in many different ways. Perhaps when the timing is right and capacity is different, more of us can contribute to causes like child hunger. But when the moment comes, I would also suggest taking time to really dig in and do research on which organization is the most effective in terms of how much money is spent on feeding the children. Resources are still going to be limiting, so you will want to know that things like education programs designed to solve the long-term problems are in place, rather than exclusively working on temporary solutions.

What we can all do, though, is recognize the small things that each of us can do today to make sure that the people around us are taken care of. We can take a meal to a friend who just had surgery. We can donate canned goods to our local food pantry. We can make sure that our own kids have food on the table, are well nourished, and get proper sleep and attention, helping them to be the best versions of themselves so they have that much more capacity to help others.

Impact Report

My immediate hope is that every one of us is inspired to take an impact report. This isn't something to share publicly. This kind of report is for you. What impacts in each of these seven seeds are you currently having? If the answer is none, that's OK! We need to start with an honest and real assessment about where we are, regardless of how far away we hope to be in the future.

I remember the first time I shared these seven groups with a friend who was a business professor, and his first question was if that was something La Terza measured annually. He was curious to know what specifically we were doing in each area, where we thought we were heading, and how we grew each year. That was a hard question to hear because we were not doing things in every area. But it was also such an important question to confront.

Not doing something in an area is OK. It's OK today, and it's OK tomorrow. We all have to begin somewhere, and this includes planning to do something in the future if today is not an option. You may also need to focus on just one of the seven seeds to begin. After reading this book and reframing how we define social impact, my hope is that you will be surprised at even the smallest impact you might be having with any of the Seven Seeds. Just by thinking through them all and taking an accurate assessment of where you may be should help you see that in some way, you are having some kind of positive impact. You may just be a one on that scale of one to a hundred, but you're doing something!

Defining Success and Setting Goals

Once you have determined where you are, you can begin to dream of where you could go and the road that will get you there. Just like we did for the Wheel of Life exercises, when thinking about plans for our businesses, we want to begin with the end in mind. With any new initiative, where do you see yourself as the project finishes? Or, another way to ask the question is, "What does success look like?" Note that how you define success will probably look very different from the way someone else does. I see this often in anyone who is starting a business. Some entrepreneurs answer the question by saying that success looks like making millions of dollars. Others may answer that success looks like providing for their families in a way that ensures their children have access to an even better life and education. Still, others will answer the question that they will feel successful when they are lying on a beach, savoring nature while only working ten hours a week in their offshore and remote office. There is no right or wrong answer here. How you define success is your choice.

The same holds true for each of the Seven Seeds. Not only is the road of social impact a journey, it's also ongoing. Let's go back to that scale of one to a hundred again. When I think about the best, most impactful organizations in the world, I'm not sure any of them has a score over ninety. There is always something more we can be doing in each of these areas. I say this not to discourage anyone, but rather to help each of us realize that there is only so much we can do individually and within our organizations. This is crucial to keep in mind as we set our success targets. We want them to be achievable. They should absolutely stretch us and push us out of our comfort zones, but they should also be something that we can truly reach. The beauty of building a sustainable social enterprise is that as your work comes to an end, you can set the organization to be passed onto the next generations. Success looks like setting and achieving different milestones of impact while also passing the torch to the next waves of social impact leaders.

Let's take a moment to pause and let you dream about what success looks like in each of the seven seeds. In each of the areas, close your eyes and visualize, what does success look like? In twenty years, what impacts will you have made in your supply chain? And with your team? How will you have made a difference in the lives of your customers and community? Will your competition respect and honor your work in your industry?

Will you leave this planet in a better place than you found it? And how will you ensure your own life—physically, mentally, emotionally, and spiritually—is in a place that is also growing and thriving to serve you and your closest relationships.

If defining success is beginning with the end in mind, then setting goals is defining the achievable steps along the way. With the pictures of success fresh in your mind, you now know where to head with your work.

One of my favorite recreational activities is road biking, and one of my favorite rides is called the Hilly Hundred. It is a two-day event that winds through one hundred miles, through foothills of fall foliage in southern Indiana. It's a beautiful ride, but it definitely is a lot of work to stay on your bike and avoid walking up any hills. I know that these hills do not compare to mountain rides around the country or in the Tour de France, but for me, these long and steep hills can certainly feel like mountains. Sometimes when I look ahead to the steepest or longest hills, it looks like there is no way that I can make it all the way to the top. The key for me to complete the ride on my bike the entire way is to keep focused on what is directly in front of me, and only pay attention to what I *can* do. When I look ahead to the hills in the distance, I begin to feel defeated before I begin. But, when I stare down at the twenty feet ahead, or think about just counting to ten while pedaling, I know I can do that. So, I do. Again, and again, and again. Until eventually the hill begins to level out and I'm at the top. And then of course, I'm able to rest and enjoy the downhill ride.

This is exactly how we should approach our social impact. The hill ahead calls to where we need to be heading. It's helpful to look up and make sure we're still going in the right direction. But it's just as helpful, or maybe even more important to look at what's right in front of you. There will be twists and turns along the way. Sometimes it even means getting off the bike to take a break and catch your breath. Over time, the point on the horizon might even change to a different point. But in order to reach the destination, we have to keep pedaling and focus on what we can do to keep moving forward.

Impact Report Survey

SUPPLY CHAIN

In what ways is my business making a positive impact in our supply chain?

On a scale of 1–10, with 1 being a low score and 10 being the best, what number would I assign to my organization's supply chain impact today? _____

What does organizational success look like in my supply chain? What do I hope to accomplish?

What supply chain goal or goals could we accomplish this next year that would raise our score by one number?

TEAM MEMBERS

In what ways is my business making a positive impact for our team?

On a scale of 1–10, what number would I assign to my organization's team culture today? _____

What do I want my organization's culture to be? How do I want my team members to feel about our collective work?

What team goal or goals could we accomplish this next year that would raise our score by one number?

CUSTOMERS

In what ways is my business making a positive impact with our customers?

On a scale of 1–10, what number would I assign to my organization's customer focus today? _____

What do I want my organization's customer focus to be? How do I want our customers to feel about our organization?

What customer goal or goals could we accomplish this next year that would raise our score by one number?

COMMUNITY

In what ways is my business making a positive impact in our community?

On a scale of 1–10, what number would I assign to my organization's local impact today? _____

What do I hope our organization will be known for within our community? How do I want our community members to feel about our organization?

What community goal or goals could we accomplish this next year that would raise our score by one number?

COMPETITORS

In what ways is my business supporting or celebrating my competition or my industry?

On a scale of 1–10, what number would I assign to my organization's interactions with my competition today? _____

What do I want my organization to be known for among my competitors? How do I want my competition to feel about me and my organization?

What competitor goal or goals could I accomplish this next year that would raise my score by one number?

ENVIRONMENT

How am I making a positive difference for a greener planet? How is our organization working toward environmental sustainability?

On a scale of 1–10, what number would I assign to my organization's environmental footprint today? _____

What do I want our organization's environmental impact to be? How can our environmental footprint be net positive? How can I personally make a long-term difference?

What environmental goal or goals could we accomplish this next year that would raise our score by one number?

SELF-CARE

How am I building into my physical health?

How am I setting time aside for my emotional health?

How am I growing in my knowledge and curiosity?

How am I protecting my mental and spiritual health?

How am I investing in my personal relationships?

How am I creating a healthy work/life balance?

On a scale of 1–10, what number would I assign to my self-care today? _____

What does the healthiest version of me look like?

What personal goal or goals could I accomplish this next year that would raise my score by one number?

IMPACT REPORT TOTALS

Add up all your scores: _____

Congratulations! You are having a positive impact with the world through your work. This assessment is a great tool to revisit quarterly, bi-annually, or annually to measure progress. Celebrate your wins with each assessment and note how you've achieved new levels of social impact.

Running a business truly is a journey, isn't it? In life and work, when you solve one problem, another always pops up. But at their very core, businesses are built to solve problems. Without problems to solve and needs to be met, companies would have no purpose at all. Look at some of the most financially successful and well-known companies: Apple helps us connect with the world easily and intuitively. Nike meets our need to protect our feet while motivating us to reach for our dreams. Whole Foods meets not only our need for convenient food, but also our desire to feel good about what we're putting in our bodies. If these companies hadn't been founded on meeting those human needs and desires, they wouldn't be as hugely successful as they are today.

Businesses solve problems and meet needs from a consumer standpoint, and they are perfectly suited to simultaneously solve our environmental and social needs as well. A natural grocery store, for example, can meet an individual consumer's need for healthy food while also working to solve our larger climate change problem. By sourcing food from regenerative farms that work to heal the soil, capture carbon from the atmosphere, decrease the use of toxic pesticides, and promote agricultural biodiversity, social issues can be addressed from the source to the consumer. This is a powerful example and why I believe that we can use the proven tools of business to help solve larger collective problems.

Now I want to be clear: I'm not saying that businesses alone will save the world. It's just not that simple. Governments, nonprofit organizations, individuals, and local communities all play an important role in solving our larger problems as well. We need policy change and effective governmental leadership. We need legal measures in place to hold companies accountable for their actions. We need the important work of activists, unaffiliated charities, and grassroots organizations. We need parents, teachers, and other caregivers to raise a conscious generation. Each person and organization has an important role to play in solving our current societal ills and bringing about a more equitable and sustainable future.

It's so foundational that all of us—no matter what work we find ourselves in, or what sector we work from—keep going back to the Golden Rule and treating each other the way we would want to be treated. If we can embody this life principle—from the first lessons we learned from the poster in our elementary school classroom—then we can usher in this new economy that so many of us dream and hope for. It's an economy of equal access; one that empowers, and a system that accelerates large social changes. I truly believe that the ideals of social enterprise could really be just that simple.

For entrepreneurs and managers, applying the Golden Rule to business means treating the people providing your product or service the way you'd want to be treated if you were doing it yourself. Pay them fairly, give them health care and paid time off, and don't lay on an overly stressful workload. It means treating the environment the way you'd want to be treated: with care and responsibility. It means treating your customers the way you'd want to be treated, by providing them with a high-quality product at a fair price point. I know that it's often more complicated than that on a practical, real-world level. But, as a social entrepreneur and business leader, I find it extremely helpful to keep this idea constantly in the back of my mind, and to return to it every time a new problem or ethical dilemma crops up: How would I want to be treated in this situation?

It's "GO time"

You've probably heard the old Chinese proverb "The best time to plant a tree was twenty years ago. The second-best time is now." While it may have become a bit of a platitude, I tend to believe that most clichés get worn out because they're not only true but also deeply and universally resonant. The time to plant is now.

Depending on what kind of business you have or work for and at what stage that business is currently operating, you may have a variety of different thoughts or feelings about taking action on each of the Seven Seeds. You may have had overwhelming thoughts like "There is no way I can achieve all of this!" Or maybe you've discovered that your business was more socially responsible than you thought! Regardless of where you and your company currently stand, each and every one of us can take one small step today. Remember: This is a journey. I invite you to join it.

My hope is that over the next few decades, we will come together to create a business world that is truly regenerative. I hope that we will not only "do no harm" with our businesses, but that we will actually restore what has been lost through extractive hyper-capitalism. I hope that we not only stop cutting down trees, but that we plant more of them—and that we not only plant new trees, but that we protect old-growth forests, too. I hope that employers not only stop exploiting workers, but that we play a contributing role in their happiness and holistic well-being. I hope that we not only stop selling customers what they don't want, but that we start offering them what they truly need. I hope that we not only tolerate our competitors, but that we collaborate with them toward our shared larger goals. I hope that we continually and intentionally take care of ourselves in the process. I dream of a world where together, we look at business with a new lens and usher in the new economy by planting one small seed at a time.

There are times when I wish I could go back and tell all of this to my younger self—the David who was still running the carpet-cleaning business. When I started, I began with what I think is a common mindset, that I should earn as much money as I could so that I could give back later in life. Part of my own journey was to give back by serving in my spare time, but I still was driven by this philosophy. I had no idea that my social impact in my business could be incorporated with much more intentionality and in so many additional ways. This lens of the Golden Rule and asking the questions on how I could treat everyone I touched in a positive way has become a guide in my business endeavors. It has reshaped my thinking about how I can make the world a better place.

Looking back now, after everything I learned, it's obvious that I was operating a social enterprise back then. I was cleaning carpets with environmentally friendly products and teaching home and business owners how to decrease the amount of toxins in their homes and workplaces! But I didn't see it that way at the time. If today I met a young David who owned a carpet-cleaning business and was eager to make a difference in the world, I would encourage him to open his mind and explore the ways he can make a positive impact right where he is. I would tell him that he doesn't own "just" a carpet-cleaning business that "just" pays his bills. I would tell him that his business is a means for change and that with it, he can do his part to help his community and the world. I would make sure to tell him that he most definitely does not have to choose between making money and making a difference.

The ideas in this book are not theoretical; they're practical. The Seven Seeds are meant to be put to work. There are plenty of "thinkers" out there—individuals who have ideas about the way the world should work and who stand on stages to talk about them. And then there are those who get down and dirty, doing the work even when it's not easy, even when there are tough decisions to be made.

My hope is that *Radical Business* can be your handbook as you do just that; that these ideas can serve as guiding principles as you work to increase the positive impact you have while running and growing your business. At times, you may find that you'll have to prioritize one area over another as you make difficult decisions. At other times, you will have to wrestle with how and when to choose immediate financial gain or long-term impact. There is no quick fix but there is a radical way of operating your business. *Radical Business* is meant to guide you on your journey.

As you embark on this journey, don't underestimate the impact you can have on other people as well. When we are treated with kindness, it's difficult to keep that kindness to ourselves. When you impact others with your business, creating a ripple effect is a very real probability. Others will see you striving to be a better human and a better organization, and when they are treated well, you are also inviting them to join the journey, creating their own impact. Many people in our supply chain are learning from each other to share ideas and have an even greater impact. As our customers learn about our passions, they begin to notice other organizations having an impact and as a result, change many more of their buying habits. Imagine how through an act of kindness, you might help a competitor begin the journey of social impact. Not only would they be encouraged to be a better competitor with you, the impact you could both have in your industry would dramatically increase. The world's beauty through social impact can grow exponentially.

I know firsthand that it's not always easy to grow an ethical and sustainable business inside our current system. But, when I get discouraged, I remind myself to return to the core message of the Seven Seeds: that small steps add up to make a big difference. I don't have to change the world overnight. All I have to do is plant the next seed. So, let's all plant together.

Acknowledgments

To my wife, Beth, who has been by my side throughout my social enterprise journey. You gave me the space to dream, to experiment, and to sacrifice, so I could reimagine what building a business could look like in a new paradigm.

To Robert Gatesi, Mike Gaines, and the rest of the La Terza team, thank you for your dedication to produce amazing coffee. You each have lived and breathed a new business model with me, through much trial and error. Your dedication to phenomenal coffee also allowed me to put my focus towards dreaming of these ideas. Without a great product, this book would not have been possible.

To Mary Allard, who helped to shape and guide our team. Through your work with La Terza and as co-host and co-creator of the Third Place Podcast, you taught me so many of the principles outlined in this book about healthy team culture and self-care. Equally important, you helped breathe life into the ideas and concepts, and brought them into reality and daily habits.

To the many entrepreneurial spirits I have encountered along the way, thank you for living your dreams and for pushing towards better social business ideas and constructs. You have challenged me to sharpen my thoughts and perspectives while also inspiring me to keep striving towards a better work life.

About the Author

David Gaines has a grounding energy that is driven by the Golden Rule in every aspect of his life. Throughout his many entrepreneurial endeavors, he has always put serving others as the highest purpose. From customers to team members, the local community, and even competitors, he continues to wrestle with the questions of how to empower the collective. Even when choices are hard and the right thing to do is the difficult, less-traveled path, David never strays from his values and has seen his businesses prosper as a result.

David also leads by example and has become a mentor and coach to many. He has a unique ability to inspire vision in those around him while also remaining balanced as a steadfast and consistent leader. His servant leadership approach has afforded him many opportunities to guide individuals and teams alike to achieve their greatest potential.

In addition to being the chief visionary and CEO for La Terza Coffee, David has served several roles within the Social Enterprise Alliance, including the board chairperson. He is admittedly an idealist who dreams of a world where all businesses are social enterprises and where people are equally valued, served, and empowered.

David is a loving husband and father, enjoys the solitude and beauty of nature, and is energized by meeting new people and old friends over a crafted beverage.